THE
PHIL HERMAN METHOD

CONTINUOUS
AND
NEVER ENDING IMPROVEMENT

PHIL HERMAN

WITH DENNIS LEBLANC

Strategy 3

Strategy 4

Dedication

This book is dedicated to Taylor,
whom I am proud to call my son,
and who is a prime reason why I strive for continuous
and never-ending improvement.
It's also dedicated to those who read this book, embrace this
concept, and who aren't afraid to put in the hard work
to grow and continuously improve.
It's a never-ending journey!

Foreword

by Bob Bohlen

Years ago, I bought a meat packing plant in St. Joseph, Missouri. Although I grew up in the cattle business, I'd never been in a meat packing plant in my life. There were three of us who owned the company. We drew straws, and I pulled the short straw. That's how I became the one who had to go run the meat packing plant in St. Joe, Missouri.

When I went there, the plant and its operations were in a tumultuous time. You see, the margin in the meat packing business is typically one-half of one percent. Raw material prices change as much as five percent in a day! Being forced to navigate this chaotic playing field was the impetus for me to learn how to develop daily accountability. Within the first month, I lost a million dollars! We very quickly figured out we didn't know very much about what we were doing. The proof was in the numbers. That was undeniable.

So that's why we developed a daily accountability, and a profit and loss tracking system so that we knew every day whether we were winning or losing. In the first 12 months after we created the daily accountability system, we went from losing a million dollars in the first month we owned it (the plant was making $200,000.00 in the previous 12 months), to earning about $10 million dollars before taxes. The accountability system was working.

Because we could see tangible results with that accountability system, we set up a second system of accountability. We had 14 cattle buyers. Every day and every week, we made a list of which buyer's cattle made the most profit. If a cattle buyer was on the bottom of the list two weeks in a row, we fired him.

That's the power of accountability. Those two accountability systems turned the company around. The plant made millions before we sold it for four times what we paid for it. I very quickly became a big believer in the impact of daily accountability.

So, you are probably wondering why I am talking about a meat packing plant in a book about real estate? While meat packing is an industry completely unrelated to real estate, the critical and powerful education learned inside that meat packing plant was transformative. It was a game changer. When I retired into the real estate industry, I just knew that same system would work. I just transferred the accountability into the real estate business.

It's simply all about holding agents daily accountable. Most agents waste 7 hours and 56 minutes of every 8-hour day by focusing on things that aren't dollar productive. The four things that are dollar productive in real estate sales are prospecting, listing, negotiating, and selling. Left to their own devices, many agents focus on the administrative part of their jobs rather than on the things that make money.

So we instilled a system of accountability, making sure our "sales" team focused on dollar-productive activities. Now, the administrative tasks still had to be done, so while we were keeping sales people on prospecting, listing, negotiating and selling, we hired and trained people that the sales team could hand off the paperwork to because agents hate detail. They hate paperwork. However, they're good at being face-to-face with buyers and sellers. We developed an administrative staff. The minute a purchase offer is accepted, the sales person passes it off to the admin or closing department. The minute they got a listing, they passed it off to the listing department, so that they could be out generating more face-to-face opportunities. It eliminates that negativity that comes from sales people doing paperwork and having to manage those steps of the process. It also gives people the chance to do the thing they do best, and the opportunity to be out there doing it all the time.

As we refined the accountability, we then worked on a business plan, then an ideal day, then what an ideal week looks like. Daily accountability incorporates all of those things into reporting to somebody you respect, a coach, who can follow you and make sure you're on track. I think Michael Jordan took tens of thousands of shots at the basket in his career. That's what makes people good, but you have to be out doing it under the guidance and scrutiny of a coach, rather than focusing on the small stuff that doesn't matter so much.

We also implement a personal and business plan so that the team members know what they're getting up every day for, what they're going to work for, and what they really want to accomplish. And it's important to celebrate those accomplishments. We use a goal reward system called 10s, 25s, 50s, and 100s. 10's are a way to celebrate having a productive and great day. It might be your favorite food, or your favorite beverage, or your favorite wine, or listening to your favorite musician on a CD in the car. A 25 is something you do to celebrate a great month, and that would be equal to 1 percent of your annual income. A 50 would be something you do to celebrate a great year, which would be up to 10 percent of your annual net income. Then, 100, which is something you want to do, be, have, hold, acquire, accomplish, or own in your lifetime. You have to celebrate those milestone accomplishments in a big way. When you lay those things in that manner, you'll see very quickly what you work for and what's really important to you.

It's very important to keep your goals and accomplishments written and tracked. If you keep track of those things, because they're written down and they're very specific, at the end of the year you'll be amazed at how many things you delete. My wife, Lillian, is the number one agent in New England. Last year, she and I accomplished 110 of 115 things we wanted to do during the course of the year. It works for coaches, too.

People who read this book may think that the daily accountability is for the benefit of the coach. It has nothing to do with the benefit of the coach. Coaching forces the student to look at what he's accomplished today and decide whether he accomplished what he wanted to do from the schedule he set out for himself yesterday. He simply marks off the things that he didn't get done today, and rolls them over to tomorrow. The key is that at the end of every day it forces him to say, "How did I do today?" On a scale of 1 to 10, with 10 being great, "Was I a '2' today or was I a '9' today?" All of my students report in that number every day. When I see a coaching student who's a '4', I then look at his sheet and say, "What's going on here?" If he's still a '4' tomorrow, I need to call him and get him back on track because I can't afford to have him waste more than two days.

Nobody can be accountable to himself. It doesn't work. It's a law of immutable physics and psychology. Here's something to consider: If you like ice cream and you weigh too much, if you're not accountable to Weight Watchers, you'll eat the ice cream. Amazing how that works. The same is true about coaching. If you're not accountable to a coach, and you're not being held accountable, you live your life just as undisciplined as you've always lived it. Coaching brings an element of discipline to the process, but the daily accountability that we've structured forces you to look at what you did today at the end of the day and decide what you're going to do to change it tomorrow. In my experience, that's a process nobody can do by himself or herself.

It's important to know how productive you are and how much time you might be wasting. The old adage is "time is money." That is so true. The amazing thing is that most people don't figure out what they earn every hour. Most people earn more than they think they do every hour. That's true if they're an employee, or a business owner running his business. Even a business owner can calculate what he makes an hour, because of all the fringes and perks. If someone who earns $20 an hour is off track for a day, that is $160 out of his or her pocket.

The real success around coaching and the real success around daily accountability is spelled: F-O-C-U-S. Focus is the key ingredient in keeping a person on track and to helping them accomplish what they want to in life. What we want them to accomplish is never ever relevant to what they want to accomplish. As a coach, you're only concerned about what your client and your student wants to accomplish.

Everybody needs a coach. Everybody needs to be accountable to somebody. Nobody can hold himself accountable, not me, not anyone else. To grow and expand, and cut down the learning time, you need a coach for that accountability. A coach can give you scripts, or dialogues, or processes to deal with life, or business, because they've experienced it. One of the most invaluable things a coach can provide is to help you shorten the learning curve, and shorten the time span it takes to achieve the success that you want to accomplish. My students can accomplish way more than they think they can. *I* know they can do that, but part of my job is translating that so that *they* can see it and feel it, and really believe it.

I have been one of the top Realtors® in the world. My wife is one of the top Realtors® in the world. We've both coached top Realtors® for the last 15 years. What we continually see is that the ones who define their targets, their goals, their objectives, both from a life perspective and from a business perspective, and are then willing to be accountable to a higher or different authority, they are the ones who have the most fun in life, accomplish the most things in life, and make the most money in life. It's absolute. It's not questionable.

I have been coaching Phil Herman for many years now. I know Phil is of this mindset because of his experience and his business career. Phil is a great student. Great students make great teachers and coaches. Phil's thirst for knowledge is unquenchable. That's why he's still out there doing battle and being the best agent he can be. If you wanted to be a quarterback in the NFL, you wouldn't want to be studying and learning the game from a team's third string quarterback who has had very little (or no time) out on the field. You'd want to be talking to Tom Brady of the New England Patriots, who's one of the greatest quarterbacks in the history of the game. Phil Herman meets the criteria of being one of the great real estate agents of all time.

The reality is, I don't know of any person other than Phil Herman out there today who has closed 7,000 plus transactions, in terms of units, and understands the problems anybody would face in real estate.

You couldn't find a better coach than Phil. That's the reason I am supporting him and cheering him on in the process. Anybody can do it providing they have the aptitude for sales. The reality is that anybody who hires Phil Herman as a coach will be lucky in their selection. He will help them make more progress than they'll ever make on their own, because he understands what it takes to get there, he is still out there on the same playing field as you are, and he understands today's real estate industry and all the things you are facing day in and day out. He is facing the same things. The difference is that he can use his experience to show you how to avoid the pitfalls, potholes and obstacles that stand in the way of your success. If you are serious about taking your career to the next level, then Phil is your coach.

Bob Bohlen
Realtor, Coach and Personal Friend

Introduction

by Greg Herder

I met Phil Herman about 25 years ago when he came to my marketing seminar in Dayton, Ohio. He stood out from all the other agent attendees because he was very intense and asked lots of very good questions and took copious notes. He wanted to learn this stuff, it was abundantly apparent. We hit it off.

Back then, Phil was already doing very well, already one of the top agents in Dayton, I think he was doing 100 transactions a year. He was a partner of one of the largest Real Estate firms in the area, and they had several partners who owned a variety of offices. They were the number one independent realty firm in Dayton.

About two months later, I did a seminar in Chicago, exactly the same seminar I had conducted in Dayton. And to my surprise, in walks Phil.

"Phil, what are you doing here?" I asked. "You know what," he said. "I've been thinking about all this stuff. I really want to make sure I'm doing this right." So he sat through the seminar again.

A couple of weeks later, he called and said: "I want you to do a branding program for me. I want to create a brand, take it to the next level." At the time, he was doing a lot of direct mail. We looked at how we could move him into some advertising and some mass media. We started a marketing plan for him, created a personal brochure, and did an advertising campaign. As that campaign unfolded, we got to know each other better. Over time, he blew up his production numbers and supercharged his career. He had grown to nearly 400 units! Pretty amazing, huh?

Phil, backed by a small team, had a month where he did 47 transactions! The following month he did 43 transactions, totaling 90 transactions in 60 days! That's what being a student of the game with a voracious thirst to learn and improve does to your production.

Phil has come to seminars of mine continuously over the past 25 years. During the first decade we worked together, he came to a seminar every six months, and was always pushing, always looking to up his game and improve his marketing and advertising.

Phil has this incredible desire to learn, and that is one of the key things that separates him from the vast majority of other agents. Phil is looking to be the best *Phil* he can be. I don't think competition with other agents necessarily pushes Phil, because Phil hasn't had any competition in Dayton for a long, long time. He's was Number One by a clear margin for a long time. He competes with himself, always asking himself: "What else can I do? How can I get better? How can I learn more?" You see this in every aspect of his life. He is incredibly healthy. He takes care of himself. He's physically fit. He eats well. He does all these things. He's always trying to *be the best Phil that he can be*.

I've had the pleasure of knowing him for all that time, and seeing him always willing to learn, always willing to try things. He has always been willing to embrace and try newer things. He was one of the first people that we built a website for; the first agent that we helped get into email marketing; and the first we did TV marketing for.

Phil has always pushed himself, thinking, 'How do I get better at marketing? How do I build my brand?' One of Phil's strengths is his willingness to take input. We work with a lot of top-producing agents, and some of them, as they have become successful, start to think they know everything. If you make a suggestion they don't like, or you suggest, "You should do your branding this way. You should change your ad this way," we sometimes get a response such as: "Well, you know, it's working fine, I'm Number One." So they don't take your advice. Often, that complacency is the beginning of hitting a plateau—or sometimes a decline—in business.

Phil has always been one to talk to us about new strategies. But he'll be honest. "That makes me nervous," he would say, "but tell me why you want to do that." If you can explain it to him, he's willing to try it.

He is very teachable and open. I think his success has a lot to do with that learning quotient. The best coaches are often the best students. Phil would push back and say, "I don't understand that, but I want to learn."

Over the years, I've recommended lots of books to him, about marketing, about different things. After he reads one, he'll call and say: " I didn't understand this part. Tell me about this. Why do you think this is right?" He's questioning and learning at every step along the way. That's truly the hallmark of Phil, because that's sort of what he does in every aspect of his life.

The average Realtor®, or even the average top producer, seems to relax as soon as he/she is supposedly Number One. They coast. But when Phil was doing 40 transactions or 50 transactions a year in Dayton, he was closing the gap on the Number One agent in Dayton, and said, "I want to go to a hundred transactions." As soon as he hit a hundred he said, "You know what? I really want to go to 200." And as soon as he got to 200, he said, "Let's go to 400."

He's always looking for, "How do I get better? How do I do it more efficiently?" Year in and year out, he has set every record there is known to man in Dayton real estate for number of transactions. He's been the Number One agent in Dayton outselling nearly 3,000 agents for 27 years straight. He's been one of the top agents for RE/MAX, for many years. He was ranked in the Top 100 agents in the nation by Realtor® Magazine three years in a row, out of about 1 million agents nationally. He's approaching 8,000 career transactions and he's still going strong, day in and day out. No matter where you look, his numbers and accomplishments are incredibly impressive. He walks the walk and knows the challenges facing agents in today's market.

If you put Phil in a marketplace like Southern California or New York, where the sales prices are dramatically higher, he would be the Number One agent on the planet by any measure. Backed by his small, efficient team, I don't think anybody comes close to Phil in doing things. He has a stellar team, which is very efficient and very driven, and that's what makes his numbers so impressive. And that's what makes him so profitable as an agent.

He's not just spending money on his marketing and branding. He spends it intelligently. He creates a media plan every year, so he knows where he's going to spend money, what it is going to be, and how it fits into his entire marketing agenda. He is constantly looking at all of those things.

One of the most impressive things about him is that as he has been growing, he has shadowed many of the top agents out there. When Phil started working with me, one of the things I suggested to him is that he spend a couple of days with Allan Domb in Philadelphia. Allan had so much business that he stopped going out to see potential clients on listing appointments and instead, invited them into his office. Phil was at the point where going out on all his listing presentations was becoming physically impossible. You can't do listing presentations constantly. And that becomes a limit to your growth as an agent. Allan started inviting people to his office or he did listing presentations on the phone.

I told Phil that he needed to see how Allen worked and to try that. Phil shadowed Allen and watched what he did, and then came back and implemented that. That one change allowed him to go to a whole different level. Phil truly has built a unique brand. Because of his consistent advertising in newspapers, his television advertising, his billboards, his direct mail, he is well known. If you need a Realtor® in Dayton, everybody knows Phil Herman. He is truly the brand of choice in Dayton, Ohio.

The number one reason an agent should hire Phil as a coach is that Phil has done it all. And he's a student of human nature. He will help anybody figure out how to improve business. I would, however, offer this one caveat: If you're going to hire Phil, you have to be prepared to work. Phil was a student who was driven to implement what he learned from others, whether it was me, Allan Domb, Bob Bohlen, or any of the agents he shadowed and learned from. And Phil will expect you to actually implement these things, and he'll hold you accountable to it. That's what great coaches do. Your reward for your focus and hard work will be a magnificent real estate business.

Phil looks at coaching as an opportunity to give back to the industry that has given him such a great life and a magnificent real estate business of his own. I think any serious agent would be absolutely crazy not to hire Phil. He truly has done every single aspect of real estate, and he is still out there doing it today. His passion for his craft is infectious, and it will inspire you.

Phil is a great coach because he has always been a student of the game, a student of real estate. His thirst for knowledge is legendary. Because of that, he can give agents advice and suggestions that are going to be far beyond what they would get in a training program from their brokerage.

The biggest challenge in real-estate training is that it's designed for the average agent, the middle percentile, and never for the exceptional agents. If you want to be exceptional, you have to go find somebody who is exceptional as well, and is willing to push you at an exceptional level. Phil is an absolutely talented and knowledgeable agent who can coach you to perform at the next level. You can build the magnificent real estate business you have been dreaming about and become an exceptional agent working with Phil as your coach.

Greg Herder
Greg Herder Training and MegaAgent Design

My Date with Destiny

"What I know doesn't concern me; it's what I don't know that keeps me awake at night."

—Phil Herman

Over the half a century plus that I have walked this earth, there is one life lesson that sticks in my mind over all others. Even though this lesson was so impactful in my life, I didn't embrace it right away. In fact, I fought it. I was in denial. Fought it tooth and nail. You probably did too.

What was this life lesson? It was the realization that I needed to rely on others. An English writer, John Donne, expressed it with his famous saying, "No man is an island…" Humans are a proud species, and even as toddlers, we pull away when our parents try to help us saying, *"I can do it myself!"*

But as I got older, I came to understand that I was NOT an island. I couldn't do everything myself. I came to understand that I relied on others to help me get through life, to help me grow, to guide me and counsel me, and to keep me on the right path in life. Parents, pastors, teachers, coaches, and best friends—these people were integral to the formation of my character and to every success that I enjoyed in life. And what is a life well lived? To me, it's *a long journey of personal growth and striving for success.*

In fact, I will say that every step, choice, and preparation we make in our lives in order to achieve success can never be determined solely by what we have orchestrated with our own hands. This is an absolute in the life of anyone who has dared to be great, who has strived for a goal. There is *always* a contributor—a person we encounter while on that journey to success that either encourages us to persevere past the failures and disappointments, or challenges us to be better than who we have been and continuously refine our efforts in our quest to excel.

Think back to your favorite teacher who helped you with a tough subject, or inspired you to learn even more about a particular topic. Think about the coach who pushed you to run another lap, to jump a little higher. Or think about that best friend, who uttered a few simple words of encouragement just when you needed them most. We need this entity, this person, to challenge us to be greater and better than we are. And that is the life lesson right there: we are not islands unto ourselves. We need others to grow and succeed. And in important times of our lives, key individuals like this play a vital role in our destiny.

New York Times bestselling author, real-estate investor, and entrepreneur Robert Kiyosaki came face-to-face with his destiny when he first met his "rich dad," as he affectionately referred to him in his 1997 book *Rich Dad, Poor Dad*. Kiyosaki described the moment he viewed his friend's father as someone whose teachings he could learn from to steer the course of his life in a direction far greater than he could do by himself. Through his initial and continuous encounter with his "rich dad" he learned valuable lessons about money, entrepreneurship, and growing a business. And within those lessons he realized that if he never changed his negative behavior, he would remain in the same position without learning and improving himself.

Kiyosaki's first encounter with his "rich dad" became his date with destiny that forever changed his life. My date with destiny happened, strangely enough, in someone's home, in a crowded living room in Southern California in 1988.

Allow me to take you back even further in order to give you a better understanding of the impact of my 'Date with Destiny,' let me take you back to 1977. I was a newly licensed Realtor® trying to convince buyers to hire me to find a home for them and sellers to place their most important investment in my hands. I was hungry, and I pushed myself and in 1984—to my surprise—I was recognized as being Dayton, Ohio's top real estate agent in a field of 2,500 to 3,000 agents. This actually came as a surprise to me because I had my nose to the grindstone taking it one day at a time and I looked up and there was this award in my lap. Truth be told, I really didn't feel as if I was applying myself enough, so I was shocked that I turned out to be the leading real estate agent. My first thought was, "Jeez, if I really dig my heels in I wonder what I *could* do." And so now I had a bar set that I had to maintain and surpass, so I challenged myself to do and be even more in my industry so that I could continue to be recognized as the best.

For the next five years I continued to lead my fellow competing agents in that board of Realtors® in number of sales transactions for the years to follow: '84, '85, '86, '87 and '88. Then, in 1989 the Dayton Board of Realtors® stopped recognizing the top real estate agent in Dayton, Ohio. A business tradition that was active for ten years suddenly ended without warning and without apparent cause. However, I knew the real reason they stopped…because the top real estate agent that sixth year would have again been me. It so happened that the other agents were complaining that they were paying board dues and not getting recognition for their work. They took offense to the Dayton's Board of Realtors® recognizing me so many years in a row as being the top agent. I thought I was paying board dues too! I felt that my continuous recognition was justified because of all the hard work I was putting in. I thought those other agents just didn't understand or comprehend how hard I work at it each and every day to be the leader in sales. In fact, it wasn't uncommon for me to work seven days a week!

I was disappointed by the news. Through those years, I had positioned myself as a successful Realtor®. I was somewhat a "student of the game," and would read books on business, marketing and advertising. I had read *Positioning*, written by Al Ries and Jack Trout. It was an influential book that talked about how being number one in a category and owning number one in the mind of the consumer is a powerful position. The concept is that when many Daytonians thought about real estate, they thought about ME, because I was recognized as the best in that field. However, I felt as if I was losing that position when they no longer would recognize who number one was. In other words, I wouldn't be able to take that to the public through marketing and advertising. It was a bit of a downfall for me. And as a result, I had a difficult time trying to figure out how to reach the public and effectively set myself apart from other agents.

So there I was, feeling that all I had worked for was no longer viable and the rewards for all that hard work were slapped out of my hands. I was not in a good place; I struggled. Then, I ran across some marketing materials promoting a training seminar being held in Southern California put on by a young guy that had just begun doing personal improvement seminars. Although I was in Dayton, Ohio in the Midwest, and it would be a far trek over to Southern California. I decided it was something I needed to attend. It was just something in my gut telling me that I needed to be there.

So in 1988 I flew nearly across the country following an intuition. I found myself sitting in the living room of this trainer on a metal fold up chair. There were about 100 other metal fold up chairs lined up in this living room of a 10,000 square foot mansion in La Jolla, California. There was a strange energy in the room; I wasn't sure what to expect as I listened to the soft murmur of all the other people sitting on these uncomfortable metal chairs. I started to doubt if my gut intuition might have been wrong. Then a tall giant of a guy walked in and introduced himself with a deep booming voice. As he stood in front of our group, he didn't look like someone who could help change my life! He was barefoot, in shorts and a sleeveless t-shirt, and said, "Hi, I'm Tony Robbins."

Then the seminar began. It was a four-day seminar that started early in the morning and went until late at night. The days were long—11-12 hour sessions. It was an immersion program, and the name of the program was **Date With Destiny.**

I was still unsure of what I got myself into. I imagined my *date with destiny* would be a beautiful woman whom I couldn't wait to meet.

My mind raced, was I really a victim to Tony Robbins' marketing and advertising, since there was no woman, just 100 other people like me sitting on those really uncomfortable metal chairs. But as I came to realize, it wasn't just 100 "bodies," it was a room filled with very interesting people, a cross section of life: a writer, CEOs of companies, stay-at-home moms, a man who was a tenth degree black belt from Japan, and many more. It was an interesting and dynamic group of people. I finally relaxed, let my guard down, stopped questioning if I had made a mistake, and I surrendered to the moment to see what I could learn. Hey, I had invested the money and the time, so what did I have to lose?

As the days went on, so did the seminar. Tony Robbins shared with us a concept I had never heard prior to meeting him. He used an acronym **C.A.N.I.** It stands for **Constant And Never Ending Improvement**. As soon as he uttered those words, they struck a chord, and immediately resonated with me. They just felt right; it was like a flash of light in my mind. C.A.N.I, Constant or Continuous And Never Ending Improvement comes from a philosophy called Kaizen, *K-A-I-Z-E-N*. Kaizen is a Japanese business mindset that evolved around the 1984-1986 time period. KAI means change, ZEN means good. (I will address the term Kaizen in more depth later in the book.)

Constant and Never Ending Improvement is all about change, change for good. From the first moment I heard this term, it became a part of my DNA. It attached itself to me. If there's any one thing that I can point to that has allowed me to have any level of accomplishment or achievement in my real estate business at all, it's having that fundamental mindset that's it's all about improvement—figuring out how to *not* remain stagnant, but instead, get better.

At that seminar, my Date with Destiny, I became a sponge, soaking it all in. I let this idea wash over me. You see, it all clicked for me in that crowded living room. Back home, I realized I did try to improve myself by reading books and talking to other successful agents. But it wasn't a focused or continuous improvement. The overall driving force as to why I had become the number one agent was that I was working like a dog, often working seven days a week! I was competitive by nature, wanted to beat the pants off my competition, but I tried to do it by working harder, not smarter.

Being competitive is sometimes driven by an urge to improve one's abilities, and sometimes being competitive is driven by an urge to work harder than your opponent. I didn't realize it, but I was paying a price for my out-of-control work ethic. It even affected my marriage. I was losing my edge; burning out. I realized that I wasn't really improving my game. My focus was more on trying to work harder than my opponents, the other agents.

You see, it all came together for me in that living room on that (really) uncomfortable metal fold up chair. I gained a new life philosophy **and** much needed perspective. I realized that I had been making a big mistake, and for a second, I felt deeply disappointed in myself for paying such a costly price. I was just grinding and grinding, mired in the trench, nose to the grindstone, mindlessly working like a dog chasing a bone, but not understanding what I was doing to my psyche. "Man, what a *huge* mistake you're making," my inner voice told me.

Thankfully, I snapped out of that momentary funk. The seminar also enlightened me to the fact that we're all going to make a lot of mistakes as we travel the journey of life. As a matter of fact, I learned that **failure is the avenue that leads to high levels of achievements**. You're going to make mistakes, but you *can* change and get better. In that living room, sitting on that metal fold up chair for four days, Tony Robbins was a spark that lit the fire in me. He gave me a focus, a life philosophy, and a center to spring from while sitting there that long weekend at a seminar in his living room in La Jolla, California. He was my inevitable "date with destiny" that forever changed my thinking and expectations for business success.

Today, Tony Robbins fills stadiums of tens of thousands of people attending his business mastery seminars and I still participate in them.

Wrestling with the Giants

For most of my life, before and during my real estate career, I was always super competitive. Being competitive requires both hard work and a desire to improve every time you step onto the playing field. I had the hard work part down pat, but my focus on the constant improvement part needed...well, it needed *improvement*. I just didn't have a name for what I had been trying to do all my life until I met Tony Robbins in 1988 and he coined the term C.A.N.I. One of the reasons it resonated within me was because of a time in my life, when I was younger and an athlete.

My sport of choice was wrestling in high school. I always excelled in sports because I was constantly looking for ways to get better at it and challenge myself. Growing up, I knew my parents wouldn't be able to afford my college education and I would have to get it on my athletic abilities. Wrestling would be my ticket to college.

But it wasn't smooth sailing. I remember getting beat my junior year and telling the high school wrestling coach that it would not happen again in my senior year. I said this to him because I knew I would improve my skills so that I wouldn't suffer the humiliation of losing to another team. That high school wrestling coach gave me a little pat on the back, a patronizing one, because he really didn't know me or my drive to succeed.

To demonstrate the kind of drive and fire in my belly—the continuous improvement—I set out to make sure I would not get beat again. It started with me physically running to school. I literally ran home for lunch, ran back to school, and then worked out with my high school wrestling team. My hard work paid off when I was accepted into the University of Dayton and onto their college wrestling team to train. And I continued to push myself to improve. My days consisted of working out with both my high school wrestling team and coaches as well as the college wrestling team and their coaches (I wanted to train with college level wrestlers, to compete with wrestlers who were better, faster than me). After that, I was lifting weights for two hours, and capping the day off with a five mile run. This was my routine every single day. Again, I saw my hard work pay off, but I understood that to excel further, I needed to work with coaches to up my game to the level I envisioned in my mind.

With this realization, I jumped into the second phase of my game plan. To get there, I had find a way to finance that second phase. So I worked in a grocery store cleaning off produce, facing inventory, and sweeping the floors. I saved every dollar I made working in that grocery store that summer. I didn't buy a candy bar; I didn't spend a dollar. With my savings, I got on a plane and flew to three of the best wrestling camps in the country. I flew to Iowa and trained in a seminar there, the same place Dan Gable—one of the most famous wrestlers in the history of the sport and now the college wrestling coach with the most wins in the history of the sport—trained. I also attended a training camp at Michigan State and was trained by a guy named Bobby Douglas, who later became an Olympic wrestling head coach. After that, I went to Virginia and learned the Granby Roll Series.

I also trained with a guy named Joe Kuntz. He was four years older than me and wrestling with the Ohio University's wrestling team, a team that happened to be seventh in the nation the previous year. He was three weight classes above me and much stronger than me. He had more maturity strength, and he challenged me to do better. From time to time, he would give me words of encouragement, and those words meant a lot to me. You see, I never really wanted to train with someone that I could beat. I always wanted to train with people that were way better than me, much stronger than me, faster, more knowledgeable, and had more maturity strength, because that's where the opportunity for growth and breakthrough would be.

I am proud of what I accomplished in my sport. I didn't earn an Olympic Gold Medal or go on to national fame and recognition, but with the help of the above coaches, trainers and competitors, I proved something to myself. I won 32 consecutive matches my senior year, 32 wins and 0 losses, going into the Ohio State Wrestling Tournament.

It was gratifying, emotionally rewarding, and self-validating. So the concept of continuous improvement had always been within me, from a young man to now. Hearing Tony Robbins utter the words gave life and a mantra to it. And that is fundamentally what it became in me—a mantra—and it still is.

Marketing with the Masters

In 1984, the Realtors® National Marketing Institute, which is the educational arm of the National Association of Realtors®, set out on a mission to try to find about fifty of the top real estate agents across the United States of America. They were putting together this mastermind group of fifty top agents who would then teach their "secrets of success" to those at the Graduate Realtors® Institute (GRI) organizations to hopefully raise the level of play of real estate agents all across the country. Within these fifty agents, no one was from each other's marketplace, so it was a very free flow of information. I found an advertisement saying that if you sold a hundred properties in a year, you should notify the association. And so I did.

That same year I had done a hundred transactions, which was a big number in 1984. A little later in my career, I personally accomplished 358 transactions in a single year, and simultaneously led a team of twenty agents, combining to accomplish a thousand transactions that same year. We now have the technology and the tools around us that allow us to do more in less time. Today, we can put purchase offers through Dot Loop and negotiate by phone. We can get signatures done in a tenth of the time that it used to take us jumping in our cars and driving to the seller's house to get their initials, and then driving to the buyer's house to get their initials on any change or counter on the contract. But I digress....

For me, getting to be involved in that mastermind group back in 1984 was like hitting the jackpot. I was the only guy from Ohio. I learned what the top agents all across the country were doing in

Michigan, then south of me in Florida, west of me in California, east in New York and the East Coast. It was absolutely mind-boggling. Our group met once a year for an all day session moderated by a man named Bill Barrett. In our meetings we covered all aspects of the real estate business, from marketing and advertising, to building teams, to listing presentations and marketing materials, overcoming objections, and the financial aspects of the business. It was an incredible program; it was like getting an MBA in real estate. That mastermind experience really had a powerful impact on me.

That stellar group of top agents from all over the country still meets annually during the National Association of Realtors® Convention. From our first meeting to now, I made a decision to learn everything possible from these marketing masters by spending a few days "shadowing" any of them that I could. That's a process where you fly out to their office and spend a day or two as they go about their normal business routine, and they teach you along the way. This way you get a crash course on how they run their business and how it has made them successful. You get to see them working in a wide variety of situations. *(If you want to really up your game, I urge you to look into this. I conduct a few shadow programs throughout the year, and enjoy teaching agents who come out to meet me in the Dayton/Cincinnati region.)*

My goal when I shadowed these successful agents is to learn how they conduct themselves, how they list, sell, negotiate and prospect, how they build teams and lead teams, and how they brand themselves. It took me four years to complete this. Keep in mind that I was constantly looking to expand my awareness and improve my skills. I was never concerned (or complacent) with what I knew. **I was only concerned with what I didn't know, because it's what I didn't know that would take me to the next level.** I had to tap into that. That shadow experience expanded my awareness of what could be done in business and how it could be done. Remember, there is always at least one other person who you will encounter on your journey to success that will teach you how or challenge you to achieve more.

Out of that experience, I saw that I was very much handling my branding, marketing, and advertising as what I call a "For-Sale-by-Owner (FSBO)". In other words, you don't want to go "For-Sale-by-Owner" on your marketing and advertising. A "For-Sale-by-Owner" doesn't know about selling a property because most of them have never done it. They're what I would call an unconscious incompetent when it comes to selling a property because they simply don't know what they don't know. They may get the job done and sell the property, but they may not sell it at a price that they could have sold it at had they reached a larger buyer market. After what I had learned from my shadowing experience with those top agents, I didn't want to continue as a marketing and advertising FSBO. It was painful to discover how much I had to learn and grow when it came to my marketing and advertising. The most painful part was realizing how much business I was leaving on the table, or not reaching, with my FSBO approach. Don't "For-Sale-by-Owner" your marketing and brand.

Then, a new drive emerged in me, I had to master my marketing and advertising and really improve in this area. I sought out a small local marketing and advertising firm. They helped me create some ads and try to get a little bit of a brand about me. Then, at a national convention, I encountered Hobbs Herder Marketing and Advertising, an agency out of California. They specialized in real estate branding for agents. I decided to attend one of their seminars and it really opened my eyes. I saw branding, marketing, and advertising as reverse prospecting where people call you up and ask you if you want to do business with them!

Climbing with the Champions

I've been in the real estate industry for 38 years now, approaching 8,000 transactions. I have climbed mountains of success learning from many champions in order to be a champion myself. However, I never stop improving because there are always peaks to conquer. I've had my head handed to me so many times in this business that I'm beginning to learn when to duck. It's only now that I think that I can get really good at this, so I have no intention of quitting. Especially not when I'm starting to get good. I look around and I see that there are so many other ways that business can be done. It's constantly changing, and it's exciting for me. You won't talk to many people who've been in this industry for 38 years tell you that they'll do it for another 30 years. Most people won't want to. The reality is that statistically 80% of the population doesn't like their jobs.

In anything in life, you've got to have a goal and know what it is you want to do with your life.

Dr. Viktor Frankl, a psychiatrist who was also a former prisoner in a Nazi German concentration camp during the Holocaust, developed a therapy out of his experience called Logo Therapy. Basically, this therapy explains that when you find enough 'whys' to do something, the 'how' becomes easy. This is especially true when you have a goal set in place and a set of mentors, champions, to help you get there.

Tony Robbins is one of my champions. In fact, I've registered for his Business Mastery Immersion. I'm still committed to programs like these because, well ... constant and never-ending improvement. I know that after completing this program, I'm going to come out of there with new dreams, new goals, new ways of thinking. In addition, learning from these champions and now *climbing* with them in the industry has enabled me to do more than just sell real estate.

I want to give back to an industry that has given my family and I so much over the years. I thoroughly enjoy coaching students and I want to teach others the many lessons I've learned. That's why I'm launching a national real estate coaching consulting business. For now, I'll say national, but I honestly believe it will be international. Real estate is real estate, whether you're in the United States of America or Canada, New Zealand, or Australia. And I know real estate. In fact, I can give nearly 8,000 points of proof that I know real estate.

I once told my son when he was very young and playing soccer, that soccer was about two things: improving because if you don't improve you're not going to be on a team or have anywhere to play, and having fun. If you're not having fun, you'll quit. I've coached my son and watched him play soccer from the age of 4 to the age of 20, including two years in college. He had a passion for it; he raised his game and he had fun doing it!

The same thing is true in real estate. It's about having fun and improving, and in order to do that, we all need coaches and a philosophy like C.A.N.I. (Constant and Never-Ending Improvement).

So I ask you:

Who are the masters of their fields you look up to?

Who are the giants in your life?

Who are the champions you need to lock on to in order to see your destiny fulfilled?

My goal is to be that individual to help lead the way for you. As your coach, I will help guide you and direct you on this journey. I've always had coaches and mentors in my life, as an athlete and through to my entire real estate career. These individuals were stronger and better than me, in order to challenge me.

If you don't have a coach, you really ought to get a coach. If you look at the statistics across the United States of America, probably 10% of real estate agents are doing 90% of the business, and over 90% of those agents doing 90% of the business have coaches and they build teams. They understand the concept of a team—the combined work ethic of a team will always surpass that of an individual acting on their own. They also understand the division of labors. A coach will be able to hold you accountable, which is what I'll talk more about in the rest of the book.

Coaches bring out the very best in us. They can see our shadow sides and our broad sides. They can see things that we cannot see ourselves and help us remove obstacles that are holding us back from success. Coaches help us to truly pursue the potential that we all have within us.

The right coach will have faced the same challenges, limits, and issues that you're faced with. Through their experiences, mistakes, and recoveries, as well as what they learn from *their* mentors and coaches, they've learned what avenues to take to overcome challenges, hurdles and objections. A true coach is hardwired to want to share that knowledge with people like you.

The reality is this: **You can't afford *not* to have a coach.** My coach, Bob Bohlen, has been the top real estate agent in the United States of America the past decade. Nobody performs at his level. In fact, he actually calls me every Monday and has for years. I'm always there for the call and I can't wait for the call because there's not been one call that he did not positively impact me, and that I wasn't glad that I spoke with him because of his integrity and his knowledge base. Talking with my coach every week has kept me on track, motivated me to achieve more and helped me to focus on what is truly important in life – both in my business and my personal life. Fundamentally, the role of a coach is to help someone attain their goal and ultimately get what they want. Remember, no man is an island. No real estate agent is an island either. Embrace the idea of leveraging a mentor and champion to lift you to the next level, which will save you time and pain, and avoid making the mistakes that most agents make as they climb that mountain toward success. Having a coach is a "no-brainer" for me as I live a life of *Continuing Improvement.*

Strategy 1

Basic Ingredients for High Achievement

*"What is the recipe for successful achievement?
To my mind there are just four essential ingredients:
Choose a career you love; Give it the best there is in you;
Seize your opportunities; And be a member of the team."*

—Benjamin F. Fairless

I often reminisce and see myself sitting in that crowded living room on those hard metal folding chairs back in 1984. It's like an "out of body" experience. When I see myself from my perspective of the *here and now*, it's strange to think that the relatively inexperienced and younger me was poised at an incredibly important crossroads in his life. There I was so many years ago, listening and sitting face-to-face with Tony Robbins. I soaked it all in and faced a pivotal, life-changing moment in my life.

Perfectly coined, *A Date with Destiny*, Tony's seminar was truly a pivotal moment on my life path and my road to success. It was exactly like that scene in The Wizard of Oz, where the Good Witch tells Dorothy to "follow the yellow brick road." There she was at the very first brick on that road, and off in the distance she could see the Emerald City. That seminar with Tony Robbins was that first strategic brick on my own yellow brick road, taking a long personal journey that I am still excitedly pursuing. It proved to be the moment where I forever changed my thinking and expectations for business success.

But it's important to remember that the moment in one's life where you reach a turning point or life change is significant in that it will produce either a positive or a negative result. Typically, in a pivotal moment, you are at a crossroads, and the path you take will bring you to your Emerald City or possibly into the clutches of the Evil Flying Monkeys, or some other negative hurdle or obstacle in your life. Luckily for me—with Tony's teaching—he lined me up with a positive perspective and road map, and I could envision my Emerald City off in the distance. I just had to take what he taught me and push myself to constantly pursue high levels of achievement.

What comes to mind for me in terms of a strategy for high levels of achievement and success really comes from a conversation that I heard while attending the Date with Destiny Seminar with Tony Robbins. A key point Tony talked about was developing a strategy of learning from the best in your particular field if you want to be successful and grow. Ding, ding, ding! It was like a bell went off in my head. *"That's what I did when I was wrestling—seeking out the top wrestlers and coaches and gleaning everything I could from them to make me a smarter, faster, stronger and more successful competitor!"*

So, after that seminar, I set out on my personal yellow brick road on a journey that lasted about three to four years. I was going to "shadow" and learn from 30 or 40 of the top real estate agents across North America. I put the wheels in motion and pursued this goal wholeheartedly.

For me, in order to gather the ingredients I needed to achieve a high level of success, it meant shadowing top agents, looking at their business models, their operating systems, and figuring out how I could bring some of these concepts that I learned out west in California, out east in New York, south in Florida and north to Michigan and everywhere in between. Then, bring it to the Midwest, into Dayton, Ohio, and put the ingredients together to bake my own "cake," if you will.

Just as the ingredients that aid in determining the success of a cake are of utmost importance, so are the ingredients that aid in determining the success of a career. Imagine you were baking a cake, all the ingredients sitting in the bowl waiting to be mixed. Once you've begun mixing and finished, and then put the cake in the oven, you quickly realize that you left one important ingredient out of the mix: eggs. Hmm, I would imagine that the cake would not turn out exactly as you had intended. That missing ingredient plays a vital role in the outcome of the end product.

Contrary to popular belief, success does not happen overnight or come in an "Instant" box where you just add water, pour, stir, and bake. Instant success? I don't think so. In fact, high levels of achievement and success take time: cultivating a strategy, gathering ingredients, and then combining those ingredients to create a type of success.

I spent anywhere from three to five days with each of these superstar agents, gleaning as much as I could from them in order to determine what ingredients they put in their "cake" to make it the best (and more importantly, deciding if it was right for *my* cake). What made them stand out and become so much more successful than all the other real estate agents across America? While shadowing these top real-estate agents, I immersed myself in the various disciplines, from marketing and advertising and branding to high impact prospecting, building teams, listing presentations, selling, working with buyers, and negotiating. One of the key things I learned from every one of those 30-40 agents was that **recruiting, training, retaining, and leading a team** are all a very big part of being dollar productive in the real estate industry.

That is, as they start to build success, each of these agents started to hit a wall where they no longer could sustain their success doing it all on their own. Continued growth and success not only required a team to help that agent manage their newfound success, the team was essential if they wanted to grow to the next level! It's actually a classic entrepreneurial trap, a mom and pop business at some point has to shed its "mom and pop system" of doing business, or it will never take the crucial next step to ongoing growth and success. Launching a successful real estate career is no different.

In addition, it takes a focused effort on the highest dollar productive activities—**listing, selling, negotiating, and prospecting**—in order to produce lasting results. These elements make the difference in getting either extraordinary results or mediocre results.

While I was shadowing the *best-of-the-best* Realtors® in the country to learn techniques, strategies, and ideas in order to set myself apart from the Realtor® pack in my hometown, I needed to pinpoint what made each of them the best. Was it an instantaneous recipe that could be ubiquitously spread to every real-estate business and every real estate market and create immediate success, or was it a far more intricate set of instructions that was determined by ingredients unique to that agent's personality, real estate market and demographic?

The two major elements that I deduced from my shadowing time were these: **run your business organization fundamentally to create profits, and perhaps just as importantly, run it to have fun**. Simple, right? Sounds pretty simple to me. I found that I didn't have to complicate things in an effort to create a successful business.

If you have a business, the way that business is measured is on profit. However, if you just make money and you don't have any fun, then it's all not worth it. It does not create a fruitful lifestyle, but rather, a lifestyle that is driven to make money and more and more of it without enjoying its benefits. Statistically, people spend one-third of their lives working in their respective jobs or businesses. So, because of this, it behooves us to find a way to figure out how to have fun with it.

The selected group of Realtors® I chose to shadow were masters at understanding the usefulness and application of these two necessary ingredients. They learned how to bring in this element of fun as an ingredient in the "cake," while simultaneously creating high levels of consistent profit. They learned how to run organizations that were repeatable, duplicate-able, sustainable, and predictable (consistent). If they didn't, it would significantly and negatively impact those two fundamental missions of making money by creating high levels of net profit and having fun as a group and as a team.

Their work environments became an extended family environment. As I spent time with each of the 30-40 agents and their teams, I noticed that the people really respected one another and supported each other, and there was no competition within their groups. Everyone celebrated in everyone else's success. It was amazing to see how much energy each group generated and how that energy fed on itself, pushing the team even further. It was quite clear that no one in these respective groups was just showing up, punching a clock and counting the hours until they were off. I saw how these star agents surrounded themselves with star players by recruiting well, putting incentives in place to retain those star players, and keeping the fun and energy going.

Anyone who knows me knows that I am a perpetual "student of the game." Whether wrestling, real estate or whatever I am pursuing, I want to be the best. I want to know what the best in any field are doing to get *them* to the top. That's why my quest to spend time with 30-40 of the best agents in my industry, as perfectly framed and inspired by Tony Robbins, was a natural progression in my journey to success.

At each and every stop along my "Realtor® Shadowing Tour," I can attest that I have walked away with at least one or two big dollar "aha moments." That is, an idea or a tip that helped me grow my business by tens of thousands of dollars each year (if not way more, as I will cover later). I spent time with Karen Bernardi, a top Coldwell Banker agent from Boulder, CO. She showed me how she recruited a local preacher onto her team, a preacher who was temporarily without a church or congregation. She explained to me that she saw how well he talked to and connected with people. A key point I learned from Karen was that she took the time to find what motivated each person on her team. She worked with that preacher, and soon had him working with a predictive dialer, setting listing appointments for her. *A predictive dialer is a telephone control system that automatically calls a list of telephone numbers in sequence, screening out no-answers, busy signals, answering machines and disconnected numbers while predicting at what point a human caller will be able to handle the next call.* She recruited another team member who was looking to get his son through college and gave him an opportunity to work two-to-three hours a day setting appointments after his other job, and he thrived and got his son through college! He had a goal, she incentivized him properly, and it was a winning combination.

One of the other stops on the "tour," I traveled to Philadelphia, PA. I spent time with Allan Domb, a highly successful and respected agent who works five-to-six high-rise condo towers in City Centre in Philadelphia. His focus, or his niche, was narrow, just these few buildings and just condos. By narrowing his focus, he became one of the country's top agents. I watched him at work in his office while I was shadowing him. First, I watched him religiously work his DayTimer®. He was so meticulously organized! When I asked him about this, he took out a huge box of several Daytimers® from several years past, all filled from cover to cover with appointments and reminders. This drove home the idea that I use to this day, that a well-run day is one of the most powerful pillars of a successful life. After all, productivity in each day is like the oil that powers your success engine.

Allan and his team also used an 8.5 x 11-inch form called "The Problem Form." On this form, his team members described a problem they were wrestling with. They met with Allen and walked him through the form. I watched him at work over the course of a day, and I witnessed how Allan met with team members who walked in with this form. "With every one of my team members' challenges," Allan explained, "there are two solutions." One solution was where Allen quickly reviewed the main related points regarding that specific problem that the team member had carefully outlined on this great form. Allan helped them solve it, telling him or her exactly the steps they needed to handle it. Sometimes, it was deemed by Allan that it was an issue too important or too complex for the team member to solve. Allan would take it and into his DayTimer® it would go. It was amazing to witness such an efficient system in action.

One of the stops on my Realtor® Shadow Tour took me to Toronto. I was to spend some time with Craig Proctor, a highly successful Canadian agent. Like most of my time spent with these phenomenal agents, my time with Craig was also jam packed with big dollar ideas. What I remember most from my stay in Toronto was what happened *after* my day spent shadowing Craig. It was 11 p.m. and after a long and tiring day riding shotgun with him, we were decompressing and resting at his office. My brain hurt with all the great things I learned from watching him work out in the field. I asked him and his marketing guy if the Expired Market was big in Toronto, as it was in Dayton. He said, "Yes, and we've been wracking our brains on how best to attack that market." What happened next was like an explosion of energy in that office as we started brainstorming ideas on how to tap into this lucrative, but difficult market.

We were brainstorming headlines, key phrases, and ideas that would jump out at someone who had just gone through a listing with an agent and that listing had expired. Someone blurted out, "Who do you call when your house doesn't sell?" as a possible ad headline (an ad headline I had used in Dayton to great success that earned me quite a lot of revenue). More brainstorming, and the words, "Sometimes, even the best homes don't sell." I can attest that this one line has helped me close *many* Expired Listings, because of the way it plays on the ego of the proud home owner who is suddenly faced with the painful realization that their home didn't sell and now they needed to put it back on the market with another agent. It was pure genius. I still remember how dog tired we were, but it was amazing how we all rallied around the energy in the room with the excitement of what we were accomplishing. For a moment there, I was part of an elite team trying to crack the Expireds code. It was such a rush. I'm here to tell you that productive brainstorming sessions have elevated my income substantially!

I have to tell you that my four-year "pilgrimage" shadowing and studying with these 30-40 top agents in the nation (and beyond) was like attending a "real estate university." I learned so many big money ideas. I learned so many ways to help myself achieve and perform at a high level—ideas and insights that I utilize to this day. I simply can't tell you how important it is to take the time to surround yourself with the top people in your field, whatever that field may be, and soak it all in. Your goal is to find out what ingredients went into their "cake" of success. Then, filter them and add the components that they use to *your* "cake" if it seems to fit your style of operations.

When your goal is to achieve a high level of success, you must make sure you have the right "ingredients" or tools in place, working cohesively. Taking what I've learned from Tony Robbins and the best real estate agents that I was able to shadow over four years, I comprised **three basic ingredients** (below) that I applied to my success goals in business. These ingredients were critical to my reaching a new level of success in real estate and ultimately as the top selling agent.

1. Clarity

Having clarity essentially means having a clear mind and knowing what you want. Clarity must be the very first ingredient to success because it is critical for you to first know what outcome you desire before you begin gathering your ingredients to "make your cake." The outcome, of course, being a new level of success. Consequently, this also means that you must first know what you want. You have to have something that you are moving towards: a goal. The more specific you are with your goal (and writing it down is the best step here to achieve that concrete understanding), the clearer you are about what it is that you want. Likewise, the more powerful that goal ultimately will be in leading you to your success.

A sports analogy would be how a pitcher and a catcher know and agree on the best place to locate the next pitch to exploit the batter's weakness. Still, the catcher places his mitt at the exact spot he wants the pitcher to locate the ball. Even though from years of practice and playing they both know the general area that the pitch must arrive at the plate, having that physical target enhances the chances that the pitch will hit the right spot and achieve the intended goal, a swing and a miss.

Setting a goal enables you to determine your core values, measure if what you're doing is getting you what you want, and then have the flexibility in who you are as an individual to change and modify the plan to get you back on track. The more specific you are with your goal, the more powerful its outcome becomes. For example, when I first got into real estate way back in 1977 there were 2500 to 3000 agents in the Dayton, Ohio Board of Realtors®. I had to ask myself a question: Who am I going to be? How was I going to set myself apart from, and differentiate myself from, all those other agents?

Way back then, I decided that my job was to help people do what was in their best interest. That is, if they were left alone, chances are they wouldn't know they should do this, even if it was in their best interest. My expertise would be focused on their best interests. The focus was never on money and on a commission, but rather it was on helping people and influencing people to make decisions for themselves that would lead them to what it is that they wanted. When you're working with the public in the real estate industry, you must diligently work to try to figure out specifically what it is that your buyer or seller wants and why they want it. Then how are they going to get it? And how are you going to contribute to that plan and coach them along? Then, how will I periodically measure how it's performing as we go along? If I take a buyer out and I show them 20 properties and they don't buy a property, well then clearly I'm off track and not listening to what they want and why they want it.

So, what is it that you want? When I'm coaching real estate students on the phone, this is the fundamental question I have for them.

What do you want? I then ask them how they are going to get it. My role is to help them get whatever that may be.

An extremely important part of the process of figuring out *what* you want in a success formula is determining *why* you want it. And if you spend enough time contemplating what you want, then you will certainly come up with a lot of reasons as to why you want it. In Dr. Victor Frankel's book *Man's Search for Meaning*, he talks about this "why factor." He states that when you figure out enough reasons why you want something, the how becomes easy. And this will be the point where you will be equipped to implement your action plan. The work comes in trying to determine why you want it. In figuring out the "why," you must also ask yourself these questions: *What is that going to mean to you? How is it going to change your life? How's it going to make you feel about yourself? What contribution are you making to society or to the community? What will this do for your family, for yourself, for your co-workers? How is it going to contribute to your industry? What significant impact are you setting out to achieve?*

There's a lot of work that is necessary to put into this "why" factor. It's an area that a lot of people don't want to spend much time in. Instead, people generally want to figure out what their goal is and then they want to jump right into a plan, but they haven't figured out why they want to accomplish whatever it is that they're setting out to accomplish. The critical part here is when you get enough reasons why to do something, the how or the action plan becomes easier, because you're so passionate about what it is that you want to do.

There was a very savvy CEO who was trying to motivate some key executives to achieve critical company goals. He understood that while these executives were incredibly loyal to his company, he knew that the company's goal wasn't as compelling as a personal goal and a generic monetary bonus wasn't as compelling as a concrete reward they could clearly envision. So, he met with two of the executives and carefully interviewed them. One of the executives, he discovered, had always dreamed about owning a Harley-Davidson motorcycle. The other dreamed of owning a white Steinway baby grand piano. Once each executive replaced the generic (but important) company goal and generic (but considerable) reward/bonus with their own concrete visions of a Harley and a Steinway, they outperformed expectations because they could envision why they were working so hard toward that important goal.

The ingredient of clarity, incorporating the "why" factor, means that putting your plan to paper is an important part of this process. This will be your action plan where you will figure out how you are going to reach that next level of success. When you are developing your action plan you are looking at both plans for business and also plans for your life. Dr. Fred Grosse, PhD Psychologist once said, "Life is primary, work funds life."

When it came to real estate for me, I knew what I wanted and why I wanted it. In turn, I also knew what I didn't want. For example, I did not want to focus on saving money or appeasing my ego by going "For-Sale-by-Owner" in my marketing and advertising. My plan at that time was to focus on changing my brand. So, I sought out the best and engaged an organization out of California that specialized in real estate advertising and branding to manage and handle my brand. They came up with a consistent, cohesive look and feel about my image, what I do, and what I stand for. They changed me from a "cardboard cutout" agent (let's face it, too many agents all look the same and sound the same when it comes to their marketing) to a real-life person with a story, and defined values. They made me into someone who was relatable to the homebuyers and sellers in the Dayton/Cincinnati region—someone they would feel comfortable trusting their important investment with.

2. Focus

Focus is the second ingredient you need to add when going after success. Clarity gives you a pristine understanding of what you want and why. Focus gives you a concerted energy to keep you on the right track toward pursuing that goal. To focus means to direct one's attention or efforts –to have a clear and sharply defined view. Through focus, you are able to figure out enough reasons why, while also figuring out the how. Focus means ensuring you are channeling your efforts toward the right things and not getting distracted with energy and time going to the wrong things, things that don't directly contribute to your success. The how, the action plan, is where the role of a coach weighs heavily to help you get what you want. It was a critical step on my journey to success in my career when I hired Bob Bohlen to coach me one-on-one. He helped me to create focus and maintain that focus in knowing what I wanted, at different levels. He kept me on track.

Part of focus is to not just know what you want, but to eliminate what you *don't* want. In order to focus, you have to eliminate distractions or anything that may cause you to not work harder and more effectively. The enemy of a super achiever is complacency. In other words, you may be achieving some semblance of success and remaining on a steady pace, however, if you become content in this steady pace it will not bring you to any higher level of success in your career. Hands down, one of Bob's biggest contributions to my success was keeping my focus on the things that mattered.

Throwing Away the "Me" Wall

Staying focused also means that I must continually improve myself. What I found was that I was being complacent looking at my "me" wall: my wall of trophies, plaques, and accolades given to me for my accomplishments in real estate. Staring at that wall everyday was in essence my patting myself on the back saying, "Oh, look at how far I've come." Focusing my attention on that wall (both figuratively and literally) kept part of my energy focused on the past, on what I had already achieved. I was hooked on needing the validation that my past accomplishments gave me. I didn't realize what I was doing to myself and my growth until the moment came when I chose to throw that "me" wall away. I had to do this in order to continually improve, get better, and grow. That's where I want to move on to now. You have to eliminate all of your focus on the past and not dwell on it.

I remember it so clearly, the day I eliminated my "me" wall. I remember I was working in my office late one night, and I just kind of sat back in my chair thinking a bit. As I looked up, I glanced at the wall in front of me to see from the baseboard to the ceiling, left to the right, including on all four walls in my office, an array of plaques, trophies, awards, and achievements that I had accomplished over the years in the real estate industry. As I sat there, I thought, "What is this? Some kind of monument to my ego?" The more I sat and looked at it, the more I came to the realization that it is very easy to get caught up in yourself. I truly believe that complacency is the enemy of a high achiever. I bolted from my chair and I wasted no time. I went and found a big fifty or eighty-gallon green lawn bag and one-by-one, I started taking all those awards and plaques off of all four walls.

I took several bags of them out, and put them in the dumpster behind my real estate office building. The next morning, Tony, who does the janitorial work for my office, brought them into me, and said, "Phil, somebody has broken into your office, taken all your awards, and thrown them out into the dumpster at the back of the building." I had to chuckle. I looked at him and said, "Tony, that was me. I did that!" He looked at me incredulously and said, "Why would you throw all your awards away? You worked for years and years putting in a lot of energy and a lot of time to be able to achieve and earn these awards!" It was true, I had invested a *lot* of time, energy and work for those plaques and awards, and it was my visual proof that I had been outselling three thousand agents year after year for 27 years in a row. I looked Tony in the eyes and I said, "I need to start every day at zero. That hunger and that perspective has gotten me to where I am, and focusing on those plaques and awards isn't going to progress me one step forward." I answered. "That's looking backward, not gazing forward."

So, I start every day at zero. I act as if I have no listings, no 'sale pendings', no buyer leads, no seller leads, no cash flow, and no money in the bank. When I begin every day at zero, it's as if I'm a brand new agent. With that kind of mentality, and that kind of mindset, I saw it as me coming out of my cave, my work cave, if you will. This forced me to get out and find listings and buyers. I had to figure out what I needed to be doing, get dollar productive, and ensure that I remain in that 20% of agents who are earning 80% of the business in our industry. (In fact, I think the industry is moving toward a scenario where 10% of agents could do 90% of the business. If you are an agent without a plan, without a focus, and no clarity, you are contributing toward the eventuality of that "10% doing 90%" scenario. As you are read this book, remember that your personal destiny is in your hands, and if you soak in what I am teaching you, like I soaked in all that Tony Robbins was teaching me, you will also be able to join the 20% club!)

Throwing away my "me" wall had a major impact on how I moved forward from that day on. If you come into my office today there is not one plaque or one award up on any of the walls in my office. There's some artwork, but there are no plaques or awards. I start every day at zero saying: "I got this day. My job is to go get a listing today, go make a sale today." That's what the day is about for me. I make this my fundamental focus every day. If you're not face-to-face with someone that can find a listing that will lead to a commission, or that can sign a purchase contract or an exclusive right to represent buyer contract that will lead to a commission, then you're not on task. You're not on track. You're not engaged in that zone, the zone that will propel you into the 20% club of agents taking 80% of the business out there.

Here's a life changing exercise: for 30 days write down everything you do at work, and do this at fifteen-minute intervals. Then at the end of that month, create an A list and a B list. The A list will be the high dollar productive activities that bring about commission income. Activities like listing, selling, negotiating, and prospecting, recruiting, training, retaining, and leading. The B list will be job descriptions for team players—basically everything else. As real estate agents, we oftentimes think that we can do everything better than everyone else, and it's just not reality. My business developer once made 479 dials in one day. The next day, he made 350 dials. Part of what came out of this consistent focus on getting on the phone and making the calls was a listed property for $650,000. As a result, his focus led to me listing another property for $825,000. He was directly responsible for generating those two listings. The commission income that came from those two listings was almost $50,000 in income! And this was all a direct result of his clarity, focus, skills, talents, and being on task, *his* specific tasks.

Take a look at your typical day. Imagine yourself as you go about your day. Are you stapling fliers, making photocopies, or other menial office tasks? Is that directly dollar productive to you earning a commission? I know it's "part of the process," but you have to look long and hard at any activities that you can pay a minimum wage to get accomplished. It's important for you to grasp this concept if you want to achieve any high level of success and be a high-level achiever!

Planning

Now, you know what you want, you've thought about all the reasons why you want it. Then the next step is to create an action plan. An action plan is exactly that, a plan of action to accomplish your goal of success. There are four elements to an action plan—**written, detailed, actionable, and accountable**. So, how does someone create an action plan? Once you know what it is you want and why you want it, then the *how* becomes a little bit easier. One of the challenges that I've seen agents struggle with over the years is that when they're writing down an action plan or a business plan, they make it too lengthy. They've practically written a book on what they want to do and they're very proud of it when it's done, but the reality of it is that they don't review it. The result is that it's too cumbersome. Especially when you get to the point where you are assembling your team.

Trying to put the right people in the right places is essential to getting your team playing well and playing together on the field. For example, a goalie in the world of soccer has different skills than a striker does. The goalie uses their hands to keep the ball from going in the net. The striker uses their feet to drive the ball into the net. Where one athlete might be extraordinary, gifted and talented with their hands, another might be gifted and talented with their feet. You can't put the gifted, talented striker back in goal, if they don't have a set of hands, and vice versa. You can't put a goalie up at striker that has a great set of hands, but is clumsy with his/her feet. The worst thing we can do, when we bring in a new team player, is put a salesperson in an operations administrative position. They'll never be happy. And vice versa. If you bring in an operations person who likes to do administrative activity into a sales position, they're probably not going to be happy (or productively successful). It is paramount to the success of your business when you put the right people in the right positions on a consistent basis.

The key is to break it down into some of the fundamental disciplines. Allow me to give you an example. I've given my entire team an action plan for success. My focus is for everyone on my team to be on the phone everyday doing high end prospecting and dealing. This involves calling Expireds, 'For-Sale-by-Owners' and past clients. These are people within your sphere of influence. Prospecting and dealing is something we do daily; it's a daily focus. As a matter of fact, everybody on my team turns in a daily accountability sheet that tells me how many dials they've made, how many people they talked to, how many appointments they set, so they're accountable to someone. Every team player, by the business design I've set up, is to ultimately spend 20-25% of their day in business development.

The idea is everyone on my team pays for themselves by the end of the year. If someone is receiving a $40,000 a year salary, they need to show me by the end of the year that they were able to bring $40,000 in commission income into the company. That's the minimum standard. Show me that you can pay for yourself through business development. If you want to do open houses, that's fine. If you want to get on the phone every day, that's fine. If you have a large church organization and you're the piano player in front of a lot of people, and you want to let them know what it is that you do for a living, and we bring in business by helping those people, that's fine as well.

The operations administrative person is not just receiving their salary or their hourly compensation. They have an opportunity for commission income in addition to their salary or hourly compensation if they are licensed. As a team leader, everybody on your team has an opportunity to be a profit center for you, the team leader, but in addition to that, it builds confidence in the team players. When I come in to the office everyday, the focus is on two things: high end prospecting on the phone and marketing and branding. Branding and marketing is like reverse prospecting to me. It's getting people—who have seen my ads, my marketing, and who know my brand—to call *us* and ask us to do business with them. Understanding and comprehending the power of branding, my friends, was a big breakthrough in my journey to success. My investment in branding, combined with my team's high level prospecting systems, catapults me to and keeps me at the top of my game!

So, in conclusion, I have cultivated a stellar Business Development/ Prospecting team. I have made a significant investment in creating and building a powerful brand. PLUS, I empower every team member (even admins, if they are licensed) to boost their salary with a chance to earn commissions by also prospecting. That is a system that brings in cash flow. That is a system that I put together through careful planning and execution. And after all, a business is measured by cash flow, by net profit. Those have to be at the very top rung of the ladder for any business. It's all about getting face-to-face. If you come in the morning and you're not face to face on appointments and you look at your schedule and don't see appointments, then your job (and your team's job) is to spend the entire day business developing so you can get face-to-face with prospects. This is the power of planning.

3. Learning From Others

It's never been what I know that concerns me, it's always been what I don't know that concerns me.

Chinese philosopher, Lao Tzu, once said, "Knowing others is intelligent. Knowing yourself is true wisdom. Mastering others is strength. Mastering yourself is true power." Contrary to what you may have been told, and as I explained at the beginning of this book, reaching out for help is a sign of strength, and not a sign of weakness. I've worked with business psychiatrists, PhD's and MBA's my whole career, looking to figure out how I can grow myself. Learning from others definitely creates an atmosphere of *continual growth—continual improvement.*

In any relationship between people, accountability is key because you'll never grow without it. And you won't ever get to where you need to go by solely relying on yourself. This is where the value of a coach is so important. A coach is someone who will hold you accountable so that you'll do what you need to do to reach your goal of success. My personal coach, Bob Bolen, holds me accountable to holding the people around me accountable. At some time in our lives, we will connect with someone who will play the role of a mentor, a coach, a trainer, a teacher, or a professor. Someone will influence you in your life to help bring you along.

Nobody gets there alone. Whether you're an athlete, an entrepreneur, a musician, or an artist, no one gets to the top alone. Not the President of the Unites States, not the CEO of a top Fortune 500 company, and not the greatest musicians or artists. They all had help along the way and someone they learned from, someone who helped make sure they were on task, on track, focusing on the right things. Reaching out for help is a sign of strength, and not a sign of weakness. I've worked with business psychiatrists, PhD's, and MBA's my whole career, looking to figure out how I can grow myself. Even today, I still read books, listen to tapes, and attend seminars. I'm even headed out to another Tony Robbins business mastery immersion program. With a childlike enthusiasm, I can't wait to see what new distinctions he has for me or what I will learn in the process. Everything that I learn strengthens me and makes me more effective and more efficient as a human being, as a real estate agent—residentially and commercially—as a father to my son, as a good leader within my organization, and as a contributor to the community.

Nothing worthwhile in life is learned on your own. The lessons learned from the people around us will multiply in your life when you develop an effective action/business plan. So how can one multiply what they've learned from others? Well, it will emerge from a personal desire and quest to become better at something that you hold valuable. A job, a relationship, a talent. For anything that you want to multiply in your life and grow, you've got to ask more and better questions about it. If you want a better life, you've got to ask better questions about life. If you want to create more gross profit, you've got to ask better questions about how to create an increased gross profit. If you want a better relationship with your wife or with your husband, or significant other, you have to ask better questions about what makes a good relationship. It's all about who you are and what you're bringing to the relationship. If you want a better relationship with your children, you've got to ask better questions about the relationship that you have with your children.

The power is ultimately in the questions. Oftentimes, it's coming up with a powerful list of questions that will ultimately lead you to extraordinary answers and insights on how to leverage yourself and grow, and get more effective and efficient in whatever it is that you want to accomplish or achieve.

Again, the process of figuring out what I wanted in my success formula first involved determining what I wanted and why I wanted it. Again, when you figure out enough reasons why, you'll then figure out how. The how is your **action plan**. This is also where a coach comes into play in helping you get what you want. It was a critical step in my career when I hired Bob to coach me one-on-one all those years ago. To this day, we have a longstanding appointment of a coaching phone call *every* Monday. On this weekly phone call, he challenges me, holds me accountable, and directs the conversation to get me to come up with questions on how I can better myself.

Accountability of Coaching

When I first started coaching with Bob, I realized that he had a bigger vision for me and for my real-estate business than I had even for myself. This is exactly what I needed. Bob was my constant source of continual improvement. How do you get better at what you do? When you have a coach who holds you accountable every step of the way! It's only then that you can really realize what you're capable of doing. Left alone on your own, it's very difficult to get through a lot of the challenging and more difficult times in your personal and professional life and to stay focused, on track, and on task.

One of our Monday morning calls involved a discussion about me acquiring my commercial designation as a CCIM (Certified Commercial Investment Member). It went something like this: "Bob, that's a commercial designation. They're recognized as being the PhD's of the commercial investment real estate field. Why do I want to go and do that?" I remember whining and complaining about it. I continued to say, "Bob, I've led the market for two decades here, as a residential agent. Why would I want to go get my commercial CCIM designation?" Bob's response to me was this, "Well, Phil, because I think over the balance of your career, getting your commercial real estate CCIM designation will make you an additional two or three million dollars in commission." His response knocked the wind out of me when I thought of the numbers. He forced me to look at things from a different perspective—a *continuous improvement* perspective. I had succumbed to complacency with being satisfied with the earnings I was getting from being a residential expert. This complacency was hindering me from even more growth, personally, professionally and financially.

"Accountability is affirming."
–Stephen Covey

Getting a skill level in commercial investment real estate was not something that was even on the radar for me. It was not something I'd ever thought about in the decades that I'd been in the real estate industry and business. Bob explained to me that there are similarities between high level achieving residential real estate agents and high level achieving commercial real estate agents. He saw something in me and my skills, and felt as if I would do very well in that arena. Moreover, it would be an additional source of income and wealth building for my business and my family's posterity.

Bob was right that it was an additional source of income. The skillsets and the skill level are very similar. I needed to learn the language of commercial investment real estate, but it became an additional source of income. An additional profit center for me that I otherwise wouldn't have even begun to pursue left along on my own. I wouldn't have done it. As a matter of fact, for decades prior to obtaining the designation, I'd always referred off any commercial buyer leads or any commercial listing leads, to commercial real estate agents. That small referral fee was nice, but the full commission was even nicer!

I set out on a task of obtaining my CCIM designation. It ultimately took me four years to get the designation. As a result of Bob leading me to engage in the commercial real estate sector and not pigeon hole myself just in the residential arena, I've sold millions and millions of dollars in commercial investment real estate.

A good coach is always challenging a coaching student to move to the next level, and to encourage them, and to give them pats on the back, but also to flat out hold their feet to the fire, and hold them accountable for taking the steps that need to be taken in order to achieve that goal. A great coach is going to motivate you to do things you don't want to do so you can get what you want. I didn't want to get a commercial designation. I'd been a successful residential agent that had led Dayton, Ohio twenty years in a row. I just didn't want to do it, even though undoubtedly, getting a CCIM commercial designation would absolutely make me a better residential agent. Bob helped me see how it was an opportunity that would grow me and my real estate career.

Very early on in the coaching process, Bob set the ground rules. If he ever asked me to do something and I didn't do it, the coaching program was over. This was his leverage on me. If I'm the student, then he's the coach. I remember once during the process, asking him, "Bob, how do you determine who it is that you want to coach?" I remember him saying, "Phil, number one, I need to like them. Number two, I need to know that I can help them. Number three, I need to know that they'll remember where they learned it." Bob wanted to be appreciated for his contribution. I think that's a need that we all have in us as human beings—the need to be appreciated.

Bob not only taught me team building skills and strategies for improving my real estate skills and increasing my income, he also taught me how to become a better person, a better human being. Coaches keep you on track and focused on achieving what you set out to achieve. They keep you focused on what you want and why you want it. They also keep you focused on your business plan, and taking massive action on the business plan on a daily basis so that your plans and goals can live as a reality. They help you pinpoint key indicators that will help you to measure if what you're doing is working and if it isn't, showing you how to have the flexibility to change and improve. That is the meaning behind the philosophy I referenced at the beginning of this book, Kaizen—to change for the better and continuously try something else that will ensure constant improvement.

Changing for the Better

I once set up a contest with my real estate team where we challenged ourselves to set 100 appointments in 30 days. (By the way, I don't know of anybody who has set up 100 appointments in a 30-day period.) And it really turned out to be a 20-day period because there are five workdays in a week. So, if we achieved that goal, then I told them we would reward ourselves in a celebration. I would take everyone to Cincinnati to this very charming Italian restaurant for dinner. They could bring their spouses, their significant others, one of their children if they wanted, and dinner would be on me. I would also give everyone ten $100 bills—each team player getting $1000 cash! This was a rousing incentive for individual success as well as a business growth. But wait, there was more! After dinner, they would then have two hours to spend that $1,000 specifically on themselves. In other words, they could not use it to pay the utility bill, purchase something for their children or their spouses, or make a car payment or a house payment with it. They had to spend it personally on themselves and get the receipts. At the end of the two hours we would meet back in a private room for dessert and we would all have a little show and tell of what we bought for ourselves and then they would have to give me the receipts. If they didn't spend all the money then, what they didn't spend would come back to me. Although, I was sure that there would probably be nothing left over.

When I first presented this contest (and incentives) to my team, they were astonished. In the room I asked everyone there, "When was the last time that any of you just went out and frivolously spent $1000 on yourself?" To my shock and amazement not one hand went up. I knew I hit on something that would be very powerful.

Everybody was excited about this massive action that they would be taking in a 30-day period of setting up 100 appointments. In the office, we had a visual board posted with everyone's name on the left side of it. Every time an appointment was set, a little mark would be put by that agent's name so we could measure and keep track of it. We measure it every day to see if we are on track. With the enthusiasm of everybody behind us, it set an inspiring tone in the working environment. And remember, this was key to one of the important principles: Make work fun! It made us more productive and injected a bolt of excitement, fun and energy into our work. Win/win!

One individual agent, left on their own, is not going to be able to set up 100 appointments in a month, but when you work with a team and collectively get a team taking that kind of massive action where each one is prospecting on the phone 20% of our day, you have a fighting chance. These are the kinds of things you can achieve. It's been a mindset for me since I've been in the business.

Way back in 1984, at the Realtor's® National Marketing Institute, which is the educational arm of the National Association of Realtors®, Bill Barrett was the moderator for a group of 50 of the top agents across the country, asking us questions about the various disciplines, marketing, advertising, prospecting, building a team, and servicing. It was eye opening for me. That group of people became a Mastermind Group that met annually. Every year at the National Association of Realtors® convention, we met outside the convention, to do our idea exchange. That's when I began my process of shadowing 30 to 40 of the "best of the best" agents across the country.

I also became involved in a program called TEC (now called Vistage), which was not real estate oriented. TEC is an organization for business owners to come together and talk about challenges, issues, dilemmas, and problems that they face in business, as well as successes that they've experienced in their industries. In some ways, it was like an additional coaching resource for me. In that group, I was the only one with experience in the real estate brokerage industry. There were franchise owners of restaurants, construction company presidents, and manufacturing company executives around me. I was looking for ideas from other industries and not just from my own industry. One of those suggestions I took away from that process was reading books. I set out on a task to read 50 books a year, and listen to 500 to 1000 Ted talks in a 12-month period. These are massive action activities that expand who you are as an individual. When you commit to doing any of these activities, you inevitably change, and you change for the better.

Understanding that a coach is an ingredient/tool specifically designed for you will help you grow, challenge you, help you to ask better questions of yourself, better questions of your business, better questions of your daily activity, better questions of your business development, of your marketing, of running a team, of developing a team, and of being a leader. A coach is someone who has chosen to invest in you, and his/her only agenda is to help you. Think of a coach as a gift you give to yourself. Personally, I can't imagine working in the real estate industry and not having a business coach.

This is what continuous improvement is all about: changing for the better. At the root of it all, everything is about continual improvement. That is the thread that has been in my world of 38 years of doing real estate and now approaching 8,000 transactions, I've surpassed 7,000, and now I'm approaching 8,000 transactions. The definitive thread through it all is **constant and never ending improvement**. It is also a very forgiving philosophy.

The fundamental question you must ask yourself is: How do you select and choose a coach that's going to bring you along? You want to select a coach you can trust your future with, someone who will know where you need to keep your focus on, someone who knows how to solve specific challenges you face in your day-to-day routine, who can see the real estate big picture. There are real estate coaches out there who have never had a real estate license, but they are coaching thousands of agents a year. These coaches can do a check in with you to see if you are on task, but they may not necessarily help you with specific real estate challenges you may face.

It's extremely difficult for them to know where and how the industry is changing (and trust me, this industry is changing mightily and you need to know the lay of the land!). My suggestion is you find somebody that has actually done it, that has actually "baked the cake" in a real world setting and can help show you how to put the ingredients together. Someone who can lead you through that path of uncertainty and give you a sense of clarity; someone to hold your feet to the fire and hold you accountable to take massive action on a consistent daily basis. Personally, I believe a good coach should have a strong real estate background. Do you think Bob Bohlen would have had the insight and knowledge to give me the strategy and advice of moving into the Commercial Real Estate Sector as an additional source of commission income if he hadn't done exactly that himself?

Bringing together the basic ingredients for life and high achievement are necessary to create that lasting end result called success. In preparation for that success, you must be decisive in knowing what you want (goals) and why it will be useful for you. This provides you with something concrete and real to move towards. The more specific you are with your success goal, the clearer you are about what it is that you want, and inevitably, the more powerful that goal will be in leading you there.

Ultimately, **continual improvement is at the core of everything we do in life.** Whether it's business, our relationships with our loved ones, our children, our coworkers, the community, or our view of ourselves, they are all centered around continuous improvement. In addition, built within the concept of continuous improvement is forgiveness—that is, learning to forgive ourselves, and *often*. I beg for forgiveness every day because I make a lot of mistakes. And when it comes to those mistakes I can either let them discourage me or challenge me to be better. This is where you recognize the importance of an action plan— to evaluate whether you're on track or not, and also to ensure that you don't beat yourself up if you do get off track. Having an action plan (along with a trusted coach) will help to steer you in the right direction and keep you on course. Armed with these basic ingredients, you will be on your way to achieving the success you've dreamed of.

Strategy 2

Becoming Your Best

(Mastering the Core Activities in Real Estate)

"Success is nothing more than a few simple disciplines, practiced every day."

—Jim Rohn, Motivational Speaker

The above quote from Jim Rohn is one of my favorites. To me, it means that success isn't always the result of a Herculean effort. It doesn't mean that you have to accomplish heroic feats to be successful. Achieving success is often actually more mundane and boring than that. And perhaps that is why it is so elusive to so many? Truth be told, you can accomplish much and build incredible wealth in real estate by mastering a few simple disciplines. It's just the hard work involved in the "practiced every day" part that holds many back. We all love the Michael Jordans, the Larry Byrds, the Dale Earnhardts, the Mia Hamms, the Serena Williams' and the Tiger Woods of the world. We revel in their achievements and accomplishments and put them on pedestals. Everyone loves a winner and we love seeing their highlight reels and demonstrations of greatness.

But even though these greats share one universal and common activity (besides having and listening to their great coaches), the media doesn't cover it. You don't see them doing this common activity on ESPN. What is that activity? It's the sheer thousands of hours spent practicing the fundamentals of their respective sports, the commitment to practice, practice, practice. These were endless days conditioning on the basketball and tennis courts, countless hours spent perfecting their drive on the golf course, or day after day practicing ball control on the soccer field. Or in my case, all those years ago, the endless drills, running, training and scrimmages for the wrestling team. The truth is, practicing fundamentals is not sexy. Put simply, it's a dirty four-letter word that puts off many people: W-O-R-K. Watching these stars "work" is as boring as having to do those drills and repetitively practicing a single aspect of one's game, day in, day out.

But in my opinion, *that* commitment and hard work is what separates the greats from the others. Much more than natural talent and skill. There are many, many naturally gifted athletes out there, but you never hear about them because they simply didn't have the commitment to do the work needed to rise to the top. It was American icon, Thomas Edison, who coined the phrase "Success is 10% Inspiration and 90% Perspiration." This is true in the sports arena and it's true in the business arena, in particular the real estate arena.

In this section, I want to focus on helping you with your core "disciplines" you rely on as a real estate agent, to help you on your quest to be the best agent you can be. First things first, you must believe that you can actually become better. The goals you have set for your personal (as well as your professional) life must be goals that you believe you can achieve. I believe there are **Four Areas of Continuous Improvement** in real estate that require your undivided attention. These areas of continuous improvement are where you need to put your focus and energies. To me, **the core disciplines of real estate that you need to master are prospecting, listing, negotiating, and selling** (closing the sale or helping a buyer get their home). The challenge is that you have to be reasonably good at all four to be a successful agent. If you are bad at prospecting, it doesn't matter how good you are at closing listing presentations. If you are a prospecting wizard but choke when you show up at your listing presentation, what good is that? If you are good at prospecting and listing, but are a terrible negotiator who can't seem to get a home sold, how will that help you? To be a great agent, you need to push yourself to excel in all of these areas.

In the previous section of this book, we learned about gathering the necessary ingredients for high achievement: *Clarity* (visualizing what you want to accomplish), *Focus* (keeping your mind trained on what you need to do to succeed) and *Learning From Others*. (Remember, this is how I started this book, our need to rely on others to grow and learn).

I also covered how to combine those ingredients to create a success formula leading to a plan of action. However, it doesn't just end there, but rather it continues. Continuous improvement is a way of life—a way to become your best. You may be wondering or asking yourself why you need to become better, especially if you are already successful in your career. Well, the truth is that complacency will only lead to stagnancy; you will never be better in your field or career if you are not willing to learn more and improve *(Don't be one of those athletes with natural skills and talents but not the drive to push yourself!)*.

What if Michael Jordan stopped all his practicing after he shot the game winning shot to propel UNC to the national championship in 1982? That's a pretty high pinnacle for an athlete. What if he felt he was good enough to not have to push himself anymore? How would his legacy have fared? Truth is, he is a prime example of the power of *Continuous and Never-ending Improvement.* He recognized that he was lacking in his defensive skills when he went into the NBA, that continuous pursuit elevated his game (and helped cement his legacy even more). It's important for you to understand that those around you that are achieving great success are doing so because they recognize the benefits of continuous improvement (and willing to do the work and endure the perspiration) and they are willing to learn from the ones who have done it. So should you.

This section is the real "meat and potatoes" of the book. I'll share real scripts, real strategies, and killer moneymaking tricks that you can go out and apply to your real estate career tomorrow to start making money. These scripts, strategies and tips have cost me thousands of hours of perfecting through practice and trial and error. They have cost me hundreds of thousands of dollars in lost deals that I didn't get until I mastered them. It cost me tens of thousands of dollars and thousands of air miles to shadow the top agents who shared or inspired many of these ideas. Thousands of dollars in books and publications, seminars, webinars and presentations I've purchased or attended. I'm sharing them here with you, just for the cost of this book.

Some may ask, why are you so willing to share these moneymakers that have cost you so much and are so lucrative? Here is why: I want to give something back to the industry that has been such an important part of my life. So many top agents have helped me, so I want to help others, too. It's real estate karma. I also know that tens of thousands of agents may read this book, but only a fraction will have the fortitude to act on it and implement it into their careers and lives. It's also one thing to read about it, but acting on it is not always so simple.

I can ask Alex Rodriguez to jot down 10 steps I can follow on how he swings the bat to hit a home run, but even if I follow those written steps to the letter, I know the odds of me hitting a home run off a major-league pitcher are absolutely zero, no matter how many pitches I take. But if Alex met with me four times a week for several months, then my chances of at least hitting a major league pitcher increases. Once he teaches me how to outthink the pitcher, how to recognize the rotational spin of the ball to anticipate where it will arrive at the plate, how to properly snap my wrists for more power, then I have at least the fundamentals I would need to put together to have a shot at hitting a home run swing under his tutelage. I am sharing these ideas because I also know that a fraction of that fraction of agents willing to act on my tips and strategies will be so committed and energized from this book, that they will reach out to me to help them rise to the next level of their careers. (After all, these are the exact people I dedicated this book to).

Prospecting

The first core area of continuous improvement in a successful real estate career is all about keeping your business pipeline flowing with leads and new business. Prospecting. This is defined as the sum of all activities you do to attract and ferret out potential and prospective business coming your way. The sad truth is that some claim the average real estate agent sells approximately 5 homes a year. Do you remember what percentage of your day that I recommend you devote to prospecting? Yes, a minimum of 20%–25% of your day *must* be spent on activities designed to attract and/or ferret out business leads and potential clients. Let's take an informal survey: What percentage of these agents who are selling five or so homes a year do you think are spending 25% of their day prospecting? Even if you are terrible at prospecting, I am quite confident that if you spend that 25% of each business day doing some type of prospecting activity (whether that's cold calling people, placing ads in Craigslist, writing and mailing a postcard, writing a letter to send to your past clients and sphere of influence asking for referrals, even stopping and accosting passersby asking if they needed an agent, or whatever it might be) you will sell more than five homes a year.

Here is the plain truth. The building of *any* business requires focus and determination on the development of a customer base through leads. Therefore, before you can begin the listing of a property, you must first generate leads to get a listing. Lead generation is an area of continuous improvement in business development through focus and scheduling. Yes, this deserves repeating: A minimum of 20 to 25 percent of your daily schedule should include lead generation, business development, and prospecting. That's the hard work. Putting that 1.5 hours to 2.5 hours on your calendar for business development, prospecting, and lead generation is the most important part of your day and week. It is the fuel behind the business—driving it to success. The reality is, if you're on a face-to-face appointment to get a listing signed, or a face-to-face appointment with a buyer to write a purchase offer, or showing that buyer a house to write a purchase offer, then it's the result of the part of your job description that requires business development.

In my experience, I've found that real estate agents have a tendency to creatively avoid this important activity and therefore sabotage themselves from getting the very thing that they want. Incidentally that's where a phenomenal coach comes into play because **a coach's ultimate job is to help the real estate agent do something they don't want to do so they can get what they want.** That's to hold their feet to the fire, keep them on track, and hold them accountable to make sure that they're doing the first phase of having a successful real estate business: setting up consistent ongoing automatic lead generation. The amount of leads they procure will result in an array of opportunities to sell more and more properties to grow their business.

The truth of the matter is that agents will go out of their way to avoid prospecting. Making cold calls sucks. Yes. Reaching out to your sphere of influence asking for business can be awkward and embarrassing to some. Spending your hard-earned cash and your time on sending out postcards is painful. Yes, it is. You are in business for yourself. But think about it this way. Would you continue to hire and keep a business development person on staff if they were ineffective and refused to even devote 20% of their workday toward doing their job? What if after one year, their prospecting efforts only derived four to six listings for you? You wouldn't tolerate that, so why do you continue to do that to yourself? For the other agents who are doing significantly better than the dismal national average, ask yourself: Are you happy at your current production? If not, then improving your Business Development/Prospecting efforts is the key to taking your business to that next level I *know* you want to hit, and your steadfast focus, or the hiring of a coach to help you, will help keep you accountable to doing that.

Lead generation in business development is the price we pay to have a standard of business success. If you don't do enormous amounts of lead generation, then you may be forced to take any listing that you go out on, no matter how difficult the potential client may be. That client may be problematic to work with. Maybe you are oil and water; maybe they have unrealistic expectations; maybe they want to over-price their home; maybe they don't want to pay you what you're worth; maybe they don't want to give you enough time to try to get their property sold into your market place. Whatever the reason, you've got to take it because you have no other viable options. If you only have one listing appointment in a month or one listing appointment in a week, then you have to get that one listing under whatever terms and conditions that seller or that buyer is going to set for you rather than you calling the shots.

Lead generation is a skill (and practice) that must be mastered. A Realtor® has no option when it comes to lead generation. No matter what other skills that you develop in your real estate practice, if you don't develop that business development lead generation prospecting skill to be able to set lots of appointments up on a consistent basis, consequently, all your other skills, abilities, gifts, and talents will be for naught. Essentially, your other skills in this career will be irrelevant because you won't have any leads to focus on. Lead generation needs to be ongoing, like brushing your teeth. It's something you do every day; not something you do once in a while. Give up the excuses you creatively can come up with to not generate leads because there are none.

Consider what your goals are for your business practices connected with your personal life: more gross income, more net income, more free time, develop a better lifestyle, spend more time with our families, time for hobbies, for growing ourselves, for working out, or reading, etc. Whatever your goals, it is paramount that you master lead generation.

Once upon a time long ago, I was consistently on four listing ap-pointments a day. This was my goal: to be on four listing appointments a day, five days a week. That turned out to be 80 listing appointments a month, 1,000 listing appointments a year. If you're on 1,000 listing appointments a year you're going to be making some money, and also having some fun. On the other hand, if you're only on 12 listing appointments a year, you're not going to be making very much money, and you're not going to be having very much fun. You're going to be living a real estate life of anxiety and stress, and suffer through spikes where you have a stretch of good months and then a stretch of bad months. This will wreak havoc on your emotional (and financial) well-being—playing on your psyche. You're up one day and down the next; you're up one week, and you're down the next.

I'll say it again. Prospecting must be like breathing. A minimum of 20% to 25% of your day must be spent on this all-to-important endeavor. It's imperative that you do consistent, high impact, high quality business development prospecting lead generation, brand image building, marketing, and advertising, social media marketing and online marketing.

There are many vendors and gurus on real estate lead generating systems and tactics out there. One guru says you must devote all your energies to cold calling and door knocking. Another will tell you that all you have to do is create a brand and market that brand. Others will tell you that all your energies must go toward focusing your attention on past clients and building referrals. Today, some will tell you that if you focus all your efforts on social media and online marketing, that's all you need to do.

Here's a key point that was instrumental in my drive toward 8,000 transactions. I never put all my eggs in any one basket. Being a non-stop student of the game, I voraciously learned every guru's technique, took in every different style and innovation in lead generation and assimilated it into my full repertoire of prospecting weapons. I did pretty well after I had created a brand image that I've built and locked in over the past 25 plus years. But even though the branding guru told me that my Personal Brochure would replace my need to door knock and cold call, I merged the two and have been hitting it out of the park ever since. Because I have an image and brand name that people recognize and trust, when I (or my team) get them on the phone, I am much more successful in converting than if I was doing a strict cold call and had to build a case as to why they should stay on the phone and listen to my pitch.

Whether it's old fashioned networking, making calls, getting my brand exposure and reinforcing it in the marketplace, or social media and online marketing efforts, a significant portion of my day, of my business budget, and my focus is on prospecting. (Yes, even as successful as my team and I have become, it's like a religion to us). Whether you are just starting out and blocking out the morning to make calls, or you are running a complex and layered marketing machine like I am, when you successfully prospect, you will inevitably be able to pick and choose which listings you want. As a matter of fact, when I'm on a listing appointment, one of the things I tell the seller is that I do this because I *want* to do it, not because I *have* to do it. Currently, I'm approaching 8,000 in transactions, so I am a believer.

Making a Memorable Impression and Capitalizing on That Impression

Prospecting is all about making an impression on the minds of potential homebuyers and sellers, and then capitalizing on that impression. You want to stand out. Stand for something. When consumers think of real estate in my area, I know that all my hard work and investments put me on the menu of a lot of those prospects more often than not. Speaking from firsthand experience, I cannot say enough how important prospecting is in the real estate business cycle. In order to make and have a lasting impression in real estate with potential clients, you'll need these necessary ingredients: Branding, Marketing, Advertising, and High Impact Prospecting.

Everything we do as a real estate team to lock in a client and sell their property involves first branding our business, marketing what we offer, advertising to draw in new clients, and high impact prospecting to keep those clients working with the team. Whatever city or country you live in whether you're in Florida, Michigan, California or New York, real estate is real estate. The fundamentals and basics of this industry are the same. Certainly, there was a period of time where we didn't have the Internet and social media, Internet marketing and online advertising, but as these new innovations and opportunities arise, you must incorporate them into your business development activities.

I steadfastly refused to put my eggs in any one *guru's* basket. Remember, my success story (and yours should be, too) is putting together the ingredients to make my unique cake of success. I didn't fly all over North America to sightsee. I spent time with the agents who were super successful in our industry in order to find out what they were doing better than me, or differently, that I could take and apply in my own business. Even though the branding experts told me I no longer needed to cold call, even though the cold call proponents told me to throw out all my branding and marketing and just dial for dollars, I knew that it would be an amalgamation of strategies that would drive me to success. The key for me was how much more powerful my telemarketing had become exactly because I had made a big impression through my branding and marketing. Creating an impression in the minds of consumers made me a better prospector.

When you make a memorable impression, you are developing your business. I'll say it one more time: My *entire* team and I set aside 20 to 25 percent of our day and our schedule to concentrate on business development, primarily on the telephone. Too many agents avoid the phone like the plague. To me, it's an essential part of my business — and my success! **And now, as promised, I am going to share one of my most powerful moneymaking ideas or strategies in my considerable marketing arsenal.**

After these important ingredients (branding, marketing, advertising) have made a memorable impression on prospective clients and are set in place, when I have a prospect on the phone, I then add my best impression ingredient: **the gift card offering.** Quite simply, this strategy was a game changer in my business. It's a powerful idea, based on the idea of reciprocity. It is a simple idea, but it's an effective one. The best way to let you see what it is and how it works is to put it in the context of an actual telephone call/script.

Here's a script example of a conversation I would have with a brand new client (in this case an Expired) when presenting them with the prospect of selling with my company in context of the gift card offer:

"Hello sir. This is Phil Herman. I'm the broker owner at RE/MAX Real Estate Specialists. The reason I'm calling is that I noticed that your listing might have expired. Was that correct or did you sell it?"

"No, it expired."

"Sorry to hear that, sir. Why were you selling? Were you staying local or moving out of the area? What were your plans?"

"We're going to stay local. We're just going to downsize a little bit. The kids are in college now."

"So, you're wanting to downsize? I'm assuming you want to sell your house before you buy another home. Is that correct?"

"Oh yeah, I most definitely have to."

"If your home sold in the next 30 or 60 days, would that create a problem for you and your family or would that be ideally what you'd like to get done? Would this be something you would want to happen with the first realtor that you listed with?"

"That'd be great timing."

"Sir, you and I haven't met, so let me just give you my 15 second elevator commercial if that's okay? I own a company. I've been doing real estate full time for over 30 years. Individually, I've been involved in about 7,000 transactions helping a seller get their home sold or helping a buyer find their piece of the American dream. Nobody in the region's ever done 2,000 or 3,000 transactions that we know of. The average realtor only does about five a year nationally, so 7,000 is a bundle. I've outsold a field of 3,000

agents 27 years straight. I have been ranked in the top 100 three years in a row by Realtor Magazine, out of a million agents in the United States. The only reason I tell you this is so that you know I'm not new to real estate. I'm not part time and I know I can help you. At least I'm in the position to get you and your family the most amount of money, in a reasonable amount of time, with the fewest problems possible.

I'm sure that's what you want. So, I was wondering. What would be a convenient time for you to come into my office to personally meet with me? That would give us a chance to get acquainted, for me to go over your needs, see if I can help you with your needs, and also, for you to see if you feel like I'm the kind of realtor you'd like to hire. Would there be a convenient time that you could come into the office?"

Normally, this is the part where the potential client will hesitate and instead, ask me to meet them at their property.

The new client mostly likely will say, "I'd rather you come out to my property and see what we've got to work with."

"I will see your property, but the first meeting, sir, is just a brief consultation. It only takes about 15 or 20 minutes. Wait, I almost forgot. Incidentally, I have a gift for you; it's a gift card."

"Oh yeah?"

That's what you must do—just wait. In other words, I have to be patient. After I tell them I have a gift for them, I just allow them to respond. The offer of a free gift leans them towards me and my business.

"Do you want to know what this gift is? I have a $100 dollar prepaid visa gift card and it does not obligate you to hire me to go to work for you. It's just a small token of my appreciation for your willingness to come into the office for 15 or 20 minutes. I'm honoring your time because that time is valuable. The best-case scenario is that I'll get your property sold. The worst-case scenario is that you can fill your car up with gas, or go to dinner and a movie on me. You've got nothing to lose. Therefore, I was wondering, when would be a convenient time for you to come into the office for us to meet for 15 or 20 minutes?"

"So, just for coming in, I get a $100 dollar gift card? Even if I don't hire you?

"Yes. Again, it's just a small token of my appreciation for your willingness to come in and meet with me. It's acknowledging that your time is valuable and you're not obligated to hire me to go to work for you. You might be wondering how I can afford to do this. Well, not every new client like yourself will hire me, but about eight out of ten clients normally do. I've got a compelling story, I've got a great office environment, I've got a stellar team behind me, and my team has effective marketing and advertising behind us. We're really good at what we do and we do it better than anybody else."

So that is how I implement the powerful gift card idea in my telephone prospecting. (Be sure to check with your local Board laws and State regulations before implementing this in your business). If only one out of ten people did hire me, I probably couldn't afford to offer the gift card promotion. I'm not saying that everybody has to do a gift card. What I am saying is that if there's an objection, if you invite somebody to come into the office and they don't come in, you must have a backup offer that makes an impression on them. (NOTE: *For most agents reading this book, you won't be able to leverage 7,000 transactions as your calling card like I do, but you can find a validating selling point to leverage. Maybe it's that your company is the leading company in the area and you can leverage its production numbers as a member of its team, or maybe you have lived in the area for 50 years and are plugged into the community, or maybe you have a unique connection to a certain market niche, whatever it is, find your leverage point.)*

Initially, a prospective client does not see what's in it for them. But I give them a gift without any obligation. This way, they can decide to come in to a meeting in my office with an enticing remuneration for coming in. I make it easy for them to say "yes" to me.

You see, everything has a price. If I land the deal with the client and sell their home with a three percent commission on the listing side of $200,000, that's $6,000 dollars. Therefore, I can afford to give up $100 for the $6,000. It's like pre-paid marketing, you see. If I don't offer the gift and they don't come in to my office, then I get nothing in return. Zero. I'm betting a $100 dollar Visa gift card on my skill/ability. I'm betting on me because I would rather bet on me than bet on the tables in Vegas. The tables in Vegas are lined up for Vegas. The tables here are lined up for me. Look, it's not that I'm cocky or arrogant or egotistical. Don't confuse that with confidence. I'm very confident in my ability, not arrogant, cocky, or egotistical. Confidence makes all the difference in the world. You see, I can *talk the talk*, but I can also *walk the walk*. That is, I'm not afraid to do the work and make it happen.

In life, there are two kinds of people: the walkers and the talkers. The talkers are a dime a dozen. The walkers are the rare gifts and jewels who have the talents and skills, but aren't afraid to add the 90% perspiration to make things happen. Which will you choose to be?

Listing

So hopefully, after reading the previous section, you are nodding your head and agreeing with me that prospecting is a huge component in the equation to your success. Hopefully, you have gone to your calendar and you've blocked out one-and-a-half to two hours of your eight-hour day for your prospecting. Remember, it must be like breathing.

That brings us to the next cycle in the real estate equation. All that prospecting is getting your phone ringing and you are now taking calls to set up a listing presentation. I don't know about you, but I live for those presentations, they are like suiting up to do battle for me, so exhilarating. I know some agents dread listing presentations, or at least the ones that they know will be painful and hard on them. Remember, because I have invested my time and money in the prospecting, I know in my mind that if I don't want to take a listing for whatever reason, I don't have to. You know how liberating that is? It's like the worker who has saved 8 months of wages in the bank. Every day they come in, dealing with a bad boss, or a bad co-worker, is more tolerable because they know they can walk away from that job and rely on their savings while they look for a better job. That makes suffering an intolerable boss or fellow employee much easier.

For the listing appointments I am called on, I don't go out on every one. If it's not priced to a level that I think I can sell the home, then I won't take the listing because I must strategize and determine whether it's worth it for me to spend a lot of my time and my energy, and a lot of my team's energy, our capital, and our resources, to try to sell a property that can't sell. Moreover, if the property doesn't sell, we don't get back our time or the money spent to market the property and service the listing.

Having closed 7,000 (going on 8,000) transactions, you can say I'm getting pretty good at this listing game. But it's important to know that behind those 7,000 successes are probably an equal amount of failures. If you are an up-and-coming agent, or doing fairly well, not closing a listing can sting and truly affect your bottom line. You need to know that even though if I whiff a listing presentation it doesn't really mean the difference between a good year or a bad year for me, it still stings to me. That's just the competitor in me, the C.A.N.I. disciple. Sometimes, when I'm on a listing appointment or on a phone call, and the client hasn't agreed or signed and says they need to think about it, I'll know if I lost it or not. And you know, a lot of times I'll pick up the phone and ask for a second interview! I'll tell them, "This is Phil Herman again. I don't think I gave you my best presentation, so I'm asking if you can give me 15 or 20 minutes before you hire an agent."

I will do this for two reasons: First, I hate to lose and want a second shot, a second chance to win it. Second, I want to learn from what I may have done wrong and improve my "script," to improve my game. That's the C.A.N.I. (Constant and Never-Ending Improvement) principle. The key is that we should want to learn from our failures. And don't beat yourself up. Want some perspective? Michael Jordan famously said, "I've missed more than 9,000 shots in my career. I've lost almost 300 games. Twenty-six times I've been trusted to make the game winning shot and missed. I've failed over and over again in my life. And that is why I succeed."

Always be looking at improving your game, tweaking your scripts, sharpening your closes. That's my advice. Prospects only care about "what's in it for them" when they are deciding whether to hire you. In my area, there are over 3,000 agents to choose from. Your area may have more, you may have less competing agents. "Why should the prospective client pick you over all those other agents?" If you can't answer that question, you're done. If you can't find an angle that gives you an advantage, you need to start working on that. Always be improving when it comes to filling your business pipeline and getting listing appointments.

The same applies to my team in my office. I mentioned that every member of my team, even the admin people are asked to spend up to 25% of their day prospecting on the phone. This is both a team building exercise and it will boost your bottom line. I share with them my scripts, and teach them to say it in their own voices. They need to know the talking points; they need to follow a script. But if it sounds like they are reading from a script, they will fail. Nonetheless, I help them learn from their misses and failures.

In fact, I will pull everyone in the office and have them listen in on one of my calls/closes so they can hear how I do it. In this way, they can learn as they "shadow" me and watch me work. They don't win them all, far from it, but they love the opportunity to be more of an integral part of the team, contribute to its success and try to earn some bonus cash for themselves! And you know, sometimes, they will get an appointment that I failed to get. Sometimes, I may call in the morning when the parent is trying to get all the kids ready for school and I get shut down. But later in the morning, one of my admins, a parent herself, gets them on the phone after the morning rush is over and the kids are out the door to school, and a connection is made and she scores that appointment. The whole team shares the C.A.N.I. spirit with me; we are all about Constant and Never-Ending Improvement.

I may not get every listing I go after, however, if I take the client's listing, I'm confident that I will get the property sold because I did my homework and I wasn't in a position that where I had to take a bad listing. But that being said, in order for me to make good on that boast and get it sold, the seller must allow me to coach him/her through the process. This is what my team and I do for a living.

The Importance of Scripts

Your job as an agent is to convince a homebuyer or seller that you are the right person to help them get the job done. It's a mixture of salesmanship, trust building and establishing a rapport. It's probably the same with you, but over the years I have crafted and honed my pitch when I get in front of a client or on the phone with them. Even though I am having a free-flowing conversation, I am actually following a very loose script that I have perfected. I know it's perfected when it doesn't sound like a script.

The right script is the key to a successful salesperson. In fact, I have taken basic admin people in my office and taught them my scripts which they use every morning when they are doing their daily prospecting (that *every* team member does in my office). In this section, I am going to share some scripts, and a couple of other very effective methods that I have use and perfected over my 30 years in the business, drawing some elements from the superstar agents I shadowed, too. Ideas and scripts validated by my over 7,000 (approaching 8,000) transactions.

The Invitation

Okay, so you get a call, a potential lead from your prospecting efforts. You need to set up the meeting. I call it the "invitation" since I have become a big proponent (as taught to me by my longstanding real estate coach, Bob Bohlen) of conducting my listing presentations as CITO's (Coming Into The Office). I used to be adamant that doing my listing presentation in my office would NEVER work. I was absolutely of the mindset that the way things worked, the law of the land, was that the agent conducted his/her listing presentation at the homeowner's house. "How could it be any other way?" I half asked/half declared, all knowingly.

Well, I am here to tell you that I have eaten a lot of crow in regard to this. Now, nearly all my listing appointments are at my office. I can't tell you how much more dollar productive this has made me, it was a game changer. Not only did I save myself a ton of hours on the road, gasoline and aggravation, but it also completely changed the dynamic of that meeting. It was now being held on my turf, not the client's turf. I am now in control, and it has revolutionized my business. I used to be able to do four listing appointments in eight hours, now I can do four in an hour. I'll explain my system more in detail later, but let's start with the invitation script. The "$100 Visa Gift Card" is the secret weapon that allows me to arrange this.

Allow me to set the stage and script for you of one of my typical listing presentations:

"Hi (insert potential client's name). First of all, I want to thank you very much for coming into my office—my home away from home. One of the reasons, _____, that I invited you into my office is that I wanted you to see that I'm viable. The first meeting is just a brief consultation. It only takes about 15 minutes. I almost forgot, but I have a gift card for you. I have a $100 dollar prepaid visa gift card and it does not obligate you to hire me to go to work for you. It's just a small token of my appreciation for your willingness to come into the office for 15 minutes. I'm honoring your valuable time. The best-case scenario is I'll get your property sold. The worst-case sce-

nario is you can fill your car up with gas, or go to dinner and a movie on me. You've got nothing to lose. Again, it's just a small token of my appreciation for your willingness to come in and meet with me. It's acknowledging that your time is valuable."

You might be wondering how can I afford to do this. Probably eight out of ten potential clients are going to hire me. I've got a compelling story, I've got a great office environment, I've got a stellar team behind me, we've got effective marketing and advertising. We're really good at what we do. We do it better than anybody else and the majority of the people hire me when they come in. So that's why I am willing to bet on me and offer my potential clients an $100 incentive because I'm confident that the vast majority will return and hire me for my services.

Once the potential clients come into my office, they see that I'm serious about my work. They can see that I don't work out of my garage or out of my basement. Here's my script:

"We've got a great office location here. As a matter of fact, this office has been ranked as one of the top individual-producing real estate offices in the country per sales associate, and since I own it, I'm proud of that. It makes me feel like we're doing something right. In today's world with the technology that's available to real estate agents and the real estate industry, a whole lot of agents work out of their garage or out of their basement. Well _____, there's no way on God's green earth that a basement environment can provide good service. I know this because when I call to show their listings they are never there to answer the phone. So, I opt to show my buyer some other listing and they buy that one. If you were one of those sellers, you would be damaged and you wouldn't even know it. I invite people like you to come into my office so they can see I'm viable, that we got this great office location with a neoclassic award-winning architecturally designed building. It's a beautiful environment. You can see that our office is open seven days a week. Our phones are manned from 8:00 in the morning until 8:00 in the evening. We don't miss a call. I invite people so they can see that I've got a team around me and the energy and the activity that's going on in

this environment. Not to mention the servicing that we provide. You get a glimpse of the administrative staff and the operational side, as well as our lead generation side and our marketing side. You can see a little bit more of who we are and what we're all about, so for that I want to thank you very much for coming into the office for a brief 15 or 20-minute consultation. Let me just start off, _____, by asking you some fundamental questions."

Then I move on to ask the seller a series of questions:

"_____, why are you selling? Are you staying local or are you moving out of the area? What are your plans?" Then I say, *"On a scale of 1 to 10 what's your motivation to sell, 1 being you're really not motivated, if it sells it sells. If it doesn't that's okay, and 10 you'd really like to see this property sell in the next 30 or 60 days. If I sell your home in the next 30 days will that create a problem for you? Will that pose a problem for you? Do you need to purchase another home? Have you been pre-qualified or pre-approved with a lender once your home sells to purchase another home? How long have you lived in the property, _____? What did you pay for it? What's the square footage of your property? What do you owe on the property? What do you owe on the first mortgage? What do you owe on the second mortgage? Describe your home to me."*

They might describe their property by saying, *"Well it's a Cape Code. It has 4 bedrooms, 2 ½ bathrooms, a living room, and a dining room. It has a great room. It has a 2 ½ car garage, a full finished walkout basement and it's on an acre lot. The home is 12 years old. The construction is brick and frame. It has gas-forced air and heat with central air conditioning."*

Then I'll say, *"Well, tell me some special features about your property or any updates that you've made to it. Any major recent capital improvements?"*

Then I would ask you, *"How would you rate your home on a scale of 1 to 10, 1 being poor condition 10 being excellent condition?"* I want to know this information because they may say their home is rated at a nine or a 10 and when I go out and look at it it's actually a five or six, so I know they have an over-inflated idea of how well they compete in the marketplace. I might need to send my staging crew out there to bring it up to where it is actually a nine or a 10. If they say it's not a nine or a 10 and they say it's a five or a six, I would ask then them, *"What would make it a 10?"* So, I can again see how they're viewing their property. Then I'll ask them, *"Is there anything positive or negative about your home that could affect the price?"* I'll ask them, *"Is your home currently listed for sale now?"* If the answer is yes, *"Well, "When does it expire? How much do you want to list your home for realistically?"* Then they give me a number and I say, *"Well realistically, what do you think it's going to sell for?"*

Then they give me a price and I say, *"Well what would happen if your home did not get that price or your home did not sell?"* Then I can hear the challenges, dilemmas behind them not getting that price or it not selling. *"What price won't you go below?"* I would like to know what their bottom dollar is. *"Do you have any other properties to sell?"* I ask because maybe there are more opportunities for me there, and not just this one. *"What caused you to call me? What was the lead source?"*

I'll continue by asking them to be specific. If I were doing this interview on the phone, which we do sometimes, I would ask these questions before I meet with them and then we ask them a second time when I meet with them. I just word the questions a little bit differently. If a staff person is setting up this listing appointment for me, they would say to that potential seller, *"If what Phil says makes sense and you feel comfortable and confident that he can sell your home, are you planning on listing your home with Phil when you meet with him?"* If they say, *"yes,"* well that's a great response. If they say, *"no,"* then we're going to ask them why not. Then we ask them, *"Have you ever thought about selling your home yourself?"* The reason we ask this is that we want to know if they're actually serious about doing a For-Sale-by-Owner and they're just using me to tell them how to stage their house and learn how to price their house, or find out how to get their property sold.

My team also asks, *"Will all decision makers be there at the appointment?"* Since we're asking these questions on the phone before I actually meet with them, imagine how much information I have before we physically meet. Then my team asks, *"Do you have any questions before Phil meets with you?"* If they do have further questions, then my team member writes it down and then we say, *"We'll be sending over a pre-marketing packet. It'll only take a few minutes to review it before you meet with Phil, but it'll tell you a little bit more about Phil's company, his philosophy on doing business, some of the things he does to bring buyers and sellers together. Would you be willing to look at that before you meet with Phil? It's very important. It'll save you time in the appointment with Phil — a good hour — if you review that for 10 or 15 minutes before you meet with Phil."*

Then they set the day and time for the client to come in and meet with me. These prerequisite questions aid in narrowing down the needs of the client (or potential client) and in focusing my objectives as his/her Realtor®. Not to mention, my team's questions also help to decipher whether the potential client is serious about selling their property or need more time to think about it.

Now, here is the magic with the CITO style presentation, which allows me the potential to do up to four listing presentations in an hour. Once the potential client(s) has been asked these questions and they agree to a meeting with me, I come into the office in the morning for our 9 o'clock meeting. I pick up their file with all of the already answered questions. It's like when a doctor steps into the office and already has a list of information about you: how much you weigh, your height, your heart rate, or your blood pressure. Essentially, I've got all the vitals right here in front of me.

By this time, I've already sent them the necessary marketing materials. And those marketing materials are basically my silent salesperson that sells me better than I could sell myself. When I walk into the appointment I'll chat with them some more about selling their property, and then I'll ask the potential client(s), *"Did you get an opportunity to read the marketing material?"* They'll say yes. I'll say, *"Based on the information in the marketing material and what we talked about today do you feel I'm qualified to sell your home?"* They say, *"Well yes, we do."* I say, *"Well great, shall we go ahead and fill out the paperwork and get the ball rolling?"* They say, *"Yes, that's great."*

Then I'll bring in one of my assistants to join us in the meeting to go over all the federal and state required paperwork with them. Then, I'll turn to my assistant and let them know what information to add to the paperwork for the amount I will list the property for, also stating the Realtor's fee amount and the terms of the listing. In addition, I never neglect to assure my client that they are in good hands with my team and me. I close by saying, *"Thank you very much for this opportunity. I feel very confident we'll be able to get the job done for you."*

Then I excuse myself from that meeting and move on to the next lead or potential client. It's not dollar productive for me to stick around and complete paperwork with the client if I can have somebody else on my team do that for me. It then means that I have more time to work on other listing presentations. In most cases, I have another appointment waiting for me right across the hall in another room in my office. So I do the same thing again: I grab their file that's sitting outside their conference room, take a moment to skim through it, and then go in and do it all over again. I can continue meetings like these from the time potential clients walk into the office, because they normally only take about 15 or 20 minutes at the very most. I can do four listing meetings in an hour, where before it used to take me eight hours to do four listings.

Doing my listing presentations this way and asking them to come to my office has allowed me to list a higher percentage of potential clients. A higher percentage of people will hire me to go to work for them and will list with me when they come into my office than if I jump out and go to their house like every other real estate agent. And a higher percentage of the people will get the appraisals done with my company (more on that below). Consequently, a higher percentage of the properties will sell. I'll have less calls from them asking questions about what we're doing, because they've come into my office and see that we know what we're doing; we've got a great structure behind us. And as a result, we'll get more repeat and referral business.

How to Take Control of the Pricing Discussion

Realtors® take listings out of desperation when they don't have lots of opportunities. And many times, those agents might cave in to the seller and agree to a selling price that this agent knows is too high. That sets up a scenario where if you cannot get the price reductions, you'll spend time and money marketing that property and still lose the listing after it has expired. That does you no good, and results in time and money spent without a sale to recoup that time and expenditures. However, when you have more leads, you are at an advantage that allows you to have a standard to where you're not going to take just any listing unless they agree to get an independent appraisal to make sure that they price it right, not over or underpriced. And you can show your clients that you have that appraisal to use as a tool in the negotiating process to get the low ball offers up.

After the initial introduction meeting, the next step will be our second meeting. I might say, *"[Client's name], today's meeting is just a brief consultation. It's a chance for us to meet, for us to get acquainted, for me to go over your needs and see if I think I can help you with your needs. But it is also for you to see if you feel like I'm the kind of Realtor® you'd like to hire to work for you. It sounds like you are, and I want to ask you a question. Have you had an opportunity to have a third party professional independent real estate appraiser come out and appraise your property for its current market value yet?"* Most times it's 10 out of 10 people who will say they have not had the property appraised. Then I'll say, *"Well _____, the only reason I ask that question is because it's recommended by the National Association of Realtors,® and we agree with it. We coordinate it for you. They recommend it for two reasons: so you can make sure you (or an agent) does not overprice or underprice your property, and also when you get an offer, you're probably going to get a low-ball offer. All buyers are* low-balling all the sellers. The Realtors® are oftentimes representing those buyers, telling them to low-ball the sellers. The only thing that's helping me negotiate these prices higher for my sellers are the independent appraisals, so whether you hire me or any of the other 3,000 agents running around, it is a critical first step. For this, my team has an order form, not a contract. It does not commit you to list your house for sale with us; it does not commit us to take the listing. It says Listing Appraisal Order Form at the top of the form. It's on carbonless paper and you get a copy of it."

When meeting with potential clients, I also make sure I am honest and upfront with them about pricing. "Sir, you're going to know that once I get the job done for you and your family, you'll know exactly how I work. You'll know that I invite people to come into my office for a brief consultation to meet with me personally. You'll know that I'm going to order a professional independent appraisal on their property to make sure that they don't overprice or underprice their property, but also to make sure that as the Realtor®, I don't do that to them. I have no ego in the pricing of your house. I want to make sure that I get you and your family the most amount of money in a reasonable amount of time, with the fewest problems possible, and that I have a great tool to use in the negotiating process. As a matter of fact, if you're interviewing other real estate agents and they do not recommend that you get a professional independent appraisal done on your property, if I were you, I wouldn't hire them. They got their ego in the way a little bit here. They think they can outperform the third party professional independent appraisers. The reality is, agents don't. Independent appraisers outperform the sellers and they outperform the realtors when it comes to pricing, and that's why I get all properties professionally independently appraised."

When I explain the appraisal paperwork to sellers, I explain it much like this. "Let's just review your appraisal paperwork. It has your name, address, your telephone number, and the property being appraised on it. It says you're requesting to get a listing appraisal to be completed on the above referenced property. It says you agree to pay 350 dollars or 500 dollars for the appraisal at the time of the inspection for the listing appraisal. It says here you'd like to have the appraiser evaluate the value estimate to reflect a *marketing time of 60 to 90 days, or market norms, because maybe market norms are 30 days or maybe market norms are six months, so you can fill in the blank or put market norms. Then it will ask you to release all necessary subject property information to the agent noted above. Then at the bottom it says, 'The appraisals completed for [your real estate company name], and the information regarding the appraisal, inspection, and evaluation will only be released to the agent. Any requests for this information must be approved by the agent."*

I explain this to them in detail because I get a little bit of a discount on the appraisals since I do about 400 of these a year, and I pass that savings on to my clients. I openly share this with them, *"Part of that is I'm ordering the appraisal. I make it really easy for the appraisers, and all they have to do is e-mail me the appraisal, so they don't have to meet and review it with you; I'll do that with you. For that, we get a little bit of a discount that you get to enjoy. It's not my appraisal, it's your appraisal, and I'll hand deliver you the original appraisal when we meet."* Oftentimes they respond and say, *"Well you mean I'm going to pay 350 or 500 dollars for an appraisal and I don't get the appraisal because it says they're only going to release it to you?"* It's necessary for me to explain it further to them otherwise they can have hard feelings. I say, *"They're going to release it to me but I'm going to deliver it to you when I come out to see your home."*

I continue by saying, *"In that second meeting, there'll be three prices. You'll have your price, I'll have my price, and the independent appraiser will have his/her professionally ascertained price. Between the three of us we should figure out where to price your property. I've always said the pricing part's the easy part. I've helped nearly 7,000 families figuring out where to price their property. The tough part's finding the buyer. That's where I have a particular gift or talent. Again, I'm very effective at marketing. I know how to tap into that pipeline of buyers and cause properties to sell. The pricing part will be the easy part. Would you like to go ahead and order the appraisal? When the offer comes in on your property, if I can't get the price up to cover $350, the cost of the appraisal, I'll give it back to you at closing. That $350 appraisal is probably going to make it up in thousands of dollars in the negotiating process. It's one of the most critical things we can do in* *this market at this time. I will order a professional independent appraisal on your property to make sure you don't get overpriced or underpriced."*

I then add, *"We took a look at a study that we completed and what we found is that when a seller sets a price on the property, they're wrong 75% of the time. We've learned that Realtors® are missing on the price of the property almost half the time. Whereas the independent appraisers are right 75% of the time. While the independent appraisers are not perfect, nobody is, they're outperforming the sellers and they're outperforming the Realtors®. That's why the National Association of Realtors® is recommending to all the sellers that they get professional independent appraisals done on their property. Again, so the seller can make sure they don't overprice it or underprice it, but also to make sure the Realtors® don't overprice it or underprice it."*

I then finish with, *"Even though I've been doing this for over 25 years and I'm pretty good at it, I have no ego when it comes to the pricing strategy of a house. My only goal is to ensure that I get the client and their family the most amount of money in a reasonable amount of time, with the fewest problems possible. As a matter of fact, I often tell my clients that if they're interviewing other real estate agents and those agents do not recommend that the client get a professional independent appraisal done on the property then, they shouldn't hire them. A real estate agent not getting an independent appraisal probably means that they think they can outperform the third party professional independent appraisers. Reality is, they don't. It is prudent and in the best interest of the agent and the seller to get a professional independent appraisal."*

Pretty powerful stuff. I follow my own advice when it comes to appraisals. I don't worry whether I'm overpricing or underpricing any seller, because I get my work checked. I make sure that I'm doing what is in the seller's best interest, and a professional third party independent appraisal is what's in the seller's best interest. I personally believe that the way I'm doing business is at the highest integrity level — and it's the best way to control and leverage what can sometimes be an emotional stumbling block for sellers who are proud of their home and may over value its worth. It allows me to be the good cop instead of the bad cop telling them their home is worth less than they think it is.

Question-Based Presentation

It used to take me eight hours to do four listing appointments. It began with the first 20 or 30 minutes in travel time to get to the client's house. Once there, I would sit in their home with them, listening to family stories about things like the apple tree that they planted in the back yard as if that had some contributing factor to the value of the property, which most times it doesn't. On these listing presentations, after the inevitable small talk, I was spending an hour going through flip charts and going through a list of instructions and selling procedures, and my excellent track record as a real estate agent. As we were both just sitting there, I could tell from looking into the seller's eyes that they were basically fundamentally bored. This would go on for a full hour. Then, it would take me another 20 or 30 minutes to get back to the office or maybe my next appointment. With a schedule set up like this, I would only get in four appointments in a day, if I were lucky. During that time, I had a real estate coach, Bob, call me and say, "Phil, get on a plane. I want you to come up and watch how I do listings." Visiting him and watching how he did listings completely changed my world and my vision.

After spending time shadowing my real estate coach, I changed how I did listing presentations. (Again, it's all about C.A.N.I., and seeing how other agents who are better than you do business.) I noticed that my coach no longer did statement-based listing presentations, which is how I was doing them, but rather a question-based listing presentation. It was a very interesting dynamic for me to observe. With a statement-based listing presentation you are doing all the talking and telling the seller what you are going to do for them. All talk, but not enough listening. Moreover, a lot of the things that we all tell the seller that we're going to do, actually don't have any impact on getting that property sold, but we feel like we need to tell them to justify our commission and because for the past 50 years, this is the way it's been done.

A question-based listing presentation is different. Essentially, whoever is asking the questions is in control of the conversation. When you're asking questions, the other person feels as if you're very interested in them. And it's true, you are. As you're asking those questions to figure out how to help them, rather than flipping charts and telling them all these things that you're going to do, they will want to listen to you more and trust your expertise.

My coach's method of listing presentations was to invite people to come into his office for a brief consultation before he would go out to their property. Basically, he would ask them to hire him to work for them before he actually began working for them. Then, his presentation in the office comprised a series of 15 or 20 questions that he would present to the seller. Within those 15 or 20 questions he would be able to determine their motivation: why they were selling their property, how important it was to them, how fast they wanted the property to sell, or whether they were willing to wait as long as necessary.

The 15-Minute Listing Presentation

I watched my coach invite people to come into his office and complete a 15-minute question-based presentation. Then, in that consultation within the office he would talk a little bit about himself, a little about his company, ask a series of questions and then he would conclude saying, "Based on the information that I presented and what we talked about here this morning, would you like to hire me to work for you? Would you like to put me to work for you?" If their answer were yes, then he would set an appointment to go out and take a look at their property. On the other hand, if their answer was no, he would try to isolate and identify what their objection or apprehension was, overcome the objection, and if he was able to successfully convince them then he would set the appointment to go out to view their property.

Life is primary.
Work funds life.
If it just so happened that he could not sway their 'No' answer and they would not commit to listing the property with him, he wouldn't push any further or make any attempt to go out to the property because there would be no point if they weren't going to hire him as their Realtor.® He knew when it was wise to throw in the towel and move on to a more promising client. It only made sense for him to see the property if they were going to hire him. Otherwise, they might be just using him for his price, for him telling them how to stage the property and how to prepare to get it sold, and shopping commission. Pretty cool stuff, don't you agree? You may not be ready for moving your listing presentation as CITO's, but you can stop doing the boring Powerpoint-fact-driven-one-hour-slide-show presentations and start controlling the scenario by asking the right questions. *(If you would like to see some of the 15-20 questions that Bob and I use, point your browser to: philhermancoaching.com/Questions)*

Negotiating and Selling (Closing the Sale)

There is no doubt about it, in our industry, negotiating is a big part of our process, and an important discipline in which you must seek constant and never-ending improvement. In the most basic explanation, your role is to represent your buyer or seller and there is a back and forth between the agent representing the other buyer or seller. The goal is to engage with the other agent and "close the deal" and help a property exchange hands successfully from one person to another. Primarily, your goal is to protect your client's best interests, but you are also working to get the best possible outcome for your client and close the deal, which is getting the property sold or getting your buyer into another home. In keeping a sale or purchase together to the successful conclusion you are negotiating and interacting with the other agent, but also interacting and advising your client to help them succeed. These two disciplines of negotiating and selling are interrelated, which is why I combine them.

However, I'm not going to delve too deep in specific negotiation strategies and principles. That's a discussion for another book. However, I will address negotiation from more of a big picture perspective. After all, it can be argued that life is a constant negotiation process. When we were younger, we haggled with our parents for special privileges or to get out of getting punished. We traded Halloween candy and swapped trading cards. We bought our first cars and went to job interviews striving for the highest salary we could get.

The same applies to your real estate career. Negotiations begin from the time you answer the phone with a potential client. Somebody calls in and says, "I want to list my property." Immediately, you're in negotiation... and competition. You better believe that you're in competition with other Realtors,® vying for that potential client's business as well. Every appointment that I'm on, I believe that I'm in competition, which means I must get my head in the game. Having the ability to be focused is a major part of negotiating. Focus is a key element in everything. It's a key element in negotiations; it's a key element when you're on a listing presentation, it's a key element when you are prospecting for new business. Focus is a key element in your workday, learning how to commit 20% to 25% of your day to business development. Focus is an essential ingredient in baking this world-class career "cake" of yours, especially when it comes to negotiating. Therefore, if you don't have it, you're not going to win.

So, as I said before, negotiating happens at the very beginning. When you're business developing and prospecting, you're in a negotiation. When you show a house, you're in a negotiation. When you write out an offer, you're in a negotiation. Lead generation, listing, selling, negotiating and prospecting are—what I consider—fundamentals in real estate that are dollar productive. And when you grow your business to the next level and build your team, you can add interviewing, recruiting, training, and lastly retaining to that list of critical fundamentals in real estate that will help keep you profitable and dollar productive. These nine essential disciplines are essential to having a magnificent real estate practice and a magnificent life in this industry.

Negotiating comes with a certain skill level that you gain through lots of practice. I've had 39 years of doing this work and I'm approaching 8,000 sales. Through it all I've learned how to read people. Most of the communication with clients comes through the unspoken word—how clients are using their words, how they're using their body, how they're looking at you, how they're holding their body, and their breathing. All of that unspoken communication is actual communication, and negotiation happens during that time as well. To be able to negotiate well, you must be able to read and communicate with the client well.

Not only are you negotiating in an adversarial mode against the other agent involved in a transaction, but you are also negotiating your client through a complicated process. In this case, the word negotiating is closer to "navigating." That is, you are managing your client and his/her emotions and guiding them through the process and to the ultimate goal, a sold home or the purchase of a home.

As I stated earlier, I help my clients reach their goals and success by coaching them, and sharing my expertise to protect their best interests. A real estate transaction is an emotional obstacle course, and you are truly helping your client negotiate that obstacle course, sometimes advising them to go against their gut instincts, and sometimes advising them to follow that gut instinct. You are helping them negotiate every twist and turn and at times, protecting themselves from themselves.

For instance, you are working with a buyer who has picked their favorite home out of the handful I've shown them, and now they want to put an offer in. The challenge is that on this $400,000 home, your buyer has offered $360,000, and the seller has countered with $375,000. In fact, the buyer is drawing the line in the sand at $360,000, letting his ego and pride (and his fear of overpaying) drive his decision making. I know this is the right home for this family, but they are at an impasse. This is one way I would help my client negotiate this last hurdle that is blocking them from getting the home they really want. I tell them, *"You're my buyer and you've looked at a lot of homes. This is the one the whole family likes. What we have is a gap of $15,000 that is preventing you from owning this home that's right for you. You may have to settle for your second choice. I've helped a lot of buyers in similar situations, and the majority of those families who 'settled' for their second pick regret that choice. The truth is that this first-choice home is the right home to build memories, celebrate birthday parties, raise your children. Years from now, you won't remember if you paid $360,000 or $375,000, but you will remember and cherish all those memories and milestones in the 'perfect home' for you. I advise my clients that buying a home is first about building memories and feeling good about your purchase, and secondarily it's about an investment. I know this market, and you won't be able to beat this house as the ideal home for you and your family."*

Ironically, I was in this same situation recently with my own home purchase. I was looking to downsize and was starting to get into the buying process, and looked at a few homes. One Friday, I was scheduled to tour and view a home I was in negotiations to list for a prospect. I walked the house and took notes, but as I did so, I kept hearing myself say, "Wow, two huge walk-in closets, I love those!" or, "This kitchen is so open and a great layout." I was really impressed with the house. I told the family where I thought the price range was and I listed the home.

I went home and I couldn't get that house out of my mind. I compared it to the other homes I had seen and it was clearly and definitely my first pick. I told the homeowners that I wanted to meet with them the next day. I toured the house again, then I sat with them at the kitchen table and told them, "I have found the perfect buyer for this home." Their eyes perked up. "No one is going to appreciate this house more than this buyer," I added. I then told them that the buyer was ME, and that I would pay them whatever they wanted for their house (so much for being a great negotiator!). The wife was in tears, and I bought it right then and there!

I had seen more expensive houses. I had toured bigger homes. But I fell in love with that home (and I would have paid more for that house). Every night, when I come home from work, I say, "Hello home, I'm home!" Months later, I still feel so in love with the home. This is why I advise my clients to go with their first pick because the emotional rush of getting your dream home and first pick is so powerful. The investment part is secondary, to me.

Sometimes, you need to protect the seller from themselves. So as I did with the buyer in the above scenario, this is how I might negotiate and manage the seller side of that equation. The buyer is at a hard $360,000 and we are at $375,000, with the danger of the deal falling apart. If my research and numbers indicated that this was most likely the best offer the seller might get and it's in the seller's best interest to accept that offer, the exchange might go like this. I would take the seller back to the reason why they called me to list, whether it was to downsize, sell to cover college tuition, because of a transfer or to move up. "You have an opportunity to have what you wanted with this offer," I would say. "You're gambling that someone is going to pay you $15,000 more. In this market, that may not happen, and if it takes me three months to find that person, you may not have a net gain. It is not worth the gamble. After this is done, you're not going to remember if it sold for $15,000 more or less, but you will be in your new property." I then advise the seller, "But be careful here that you don't get caught up in a number. I may not be able to find a buyer with the price you want right away. I don't know what's going to happen."

Clients can be their own worst enemies sometimes. Take For-Sale-By-Owners for example. They have decided they don't want to pay an agent a sales commission. They want to save that money. But as stated, a FSBO doesn't know what they don't know, and their decision could end up costing them much more than the agent's commission. We know that studies show that many of the FSBO's eventually end up in the hands of an agent. The homeowner may not know that, and that could cost him/her. Homeowners are proud of their homes and they often let that pride cloud their judgment. They may think their home is worth $400,000 when I know it should be priced in the low to mid $300,000's. If you ask them why they think it should be priced at $400,000, they might tell you it's because we put a pool in the back-yard and that's worth $150,000. Well, I have to explain to them that sometimes the things sellers do to their homes that they think makes it more saleable, or show better, aren't always valuable. In my neck of the woods in Dayton, Ohio, the days that you can actually use that pool are very limited. And the potential buyer will most likely not share their infatuation with that pool. Another example is that for a lot of people, dogs are part of the immediate family, and trying to show a home with dogs on location can be problematic and hinder the sale. The dog smell that the home owner has become immune to, or the fact that a potential buyer who might love the house will be put off by the barking dogs and uncomfortable feeling they get while viewing the home, could be the deal killers that cost the seller.

Yes, a big part of our industry is all about mastering the art of ne-gotiating and managing all the various components and emotions that control our clients, and therefore control the transaction. When you practice your disciplines, you can become a better agent and get more leads that turn into more listings that you use your negotiating and selling skills to guide the transaction to a successful conclusion, generating referrals and return clients. It all comes back to C.A.N.I., Continuous and Never-ending Improvement. That's how you have a magnificent real estate practice and a magnificent life in this industry.

Leading

For those who take my advice to heart and study those who are the best in their field, and go to school on better agents than themselves, as well as focus on C.A.N.I. in their careers and day-to-day routines and processes, their business will grow. Moreover, their focus must be on building and leading a team because one can't manage all that new business on one's own. It's physically and mentally impossible. So, the next phase in your career is all about starting that team, and more importantly, *leading* that team. I will cover team strategies and team building in the next section extensively, but I want to touch on that concept briefly here.

In order to continuously improve, we must learn to lead—and lead well. We learn the tools of being an effective leader from the leaders around us. Besides Tony Robbins, a great leader that I have learned many lessons from is Dr. Fred Grosse. I learned from him that: *Life is primary. Work funds life.* When it comes to real estate, your main focus should be on dollar productive activity. We have discussed these previously in this chapter: listing, selling, negotiating, prospecting, interviewing, recruiting, training, retaining, and leading the team. He also said that we were all born to live like royalty. There's no honor in poverty. I'll never forget the first time I heard Dr. Grosse speak, his words have resonated with me ever since. They have become my mantra. I've been around a lot of great people, a lot of high achievers, and I've been a sponge. After 30 plus years, I'm approaching 8,000 real estate transactions. Along the way, I've had my head handed to me so many times that I'm beginning to learn when to duck. It's only now that I think I can get really good at this.

As the leader of a team of real estate agents, I am the visionary. I put the mission and the vision in place, setting the standards and setting the pace. We spend more time in our office environments than we do in our homes with our own loved ones and children. Who you surround yourself with in your home away from home, which is what I call my office environment, is absolutely important, critical, and essential. Make sure that you surround yourself with people that not only have the skills, abilities, gifts and talents you need to continuously improve your business, but also people who you like and who like you, that you enjoy being around and they enjoy being around you because you're going to be around them a whole lot. Inevitably, you're going to develop certain levels of relationships with them. You will know their spouses; how many kids they have and their children's names. But this is the kind of relationship you want to have with your team members, and you want them to trust you as their leader. People will do more for you and with you if you're treating them the way they deserve to be treated. And you want to be treated with dignity and respect, kindness and compassion.

These are critical elements to building a team. You're not just trying to get a butt in a seat; you're trying to find a chemistry and a kind of person that you feel will mesh with your existing team, your existing home away from home family team. There isn't anything I won't do for them because they'll do anything for me as my first line of service. If the public is calling and they're upset about something, certainly I want to handle it, but I'm here to protect my team players, as well. I know how hard they work for me. I understand the life energy that they put into this work and the sacrifices that they make to be in here and to play in this game of the real estate world with me.

Leading also means that you have to remain relevant. When you stop, then what? Everything else stops. So, you've got to stay relevant— engaged. You must also bring a contribution to your community and make a difference. It's part of why I've launched a national real estate coaching company. I want to remain relevant and give back. I want to lift people up. I want to help teach real estate agents all across the nation, all across the planet, how they can make more money in less time, with less struggle, less effort, and sprinkling in a little more fun, play, adventure and joy along the way. Real estate agents don't need to make the mistakes that I've made in my journey toward 8,000 transactions, and I can assist them in circumventing some of these mistakes.

Like an effective leader, a good coach can help guide you and it's imperative that you find a coach that has experience in the field. You want a coach who can *talk the talk as well as walk the walk*. There's a difference in the walkers and the talkers. The talkers are a dime a dozen. The walkers are the rare gifts and jewels. My coach has done over

10,000 transactions. That's why I hired him. I wouldn't hire him if he'd only done 200 or 300 in his career. You tell me you've done 10,000 transactions and you have my attention; you're in the game.

What was first introduced to me by Tony Robbins in 1988 about continuously improving and changing for the good and the better has become a part of my DNA. It's what drives me and what gets me out of bed. The world has opened up for me after learning from so many great leaders in this industry. I'm re-energized, re-excited about the business and its possibilities, and excited about helping others tap into their individual successes.

In his book, *7 Steps to Living at Your Full Potential*, Pastor Joel Osteen made a bold statement. He said, "To live your best life now, you must start looking at life through eyes of faith, seeing yourself rising to new levels. See your business taking off. See your family prospering. See your dreams coming to pass. You must conceive it and believe it is possible if you ever hope to experience it." Becoming your best may seem like a concept that is arbitrary or based in theory alone. Rest assured, it is not. Becoming your best is essential to every human being in any and every walk of life or career. I count it a great privilege to be afforded the opportunity to continuously improve; to learn from experts like my coach who has done it before me so that I can build my business. He has the experience and wherewithal to train me through it all. I hired him because he was the best, and I saw how I could become my best self with his help. So, I challenge you to become *your* best and "see" yourself achieving great success.

Strategy 3

Building Your Team

"If your actions inspire others to dream more, learn more, do more and become more, you are a leader."

— John Quincy Adams

Building a successful real estate career is just like building a successful business. That being said, so many agents don't treat their careers as a business. Instead, they flounder with big months, slow months and their lives and careers are more of a roller coaster ride than a successful *going concern*. One of this book's main purposes is to help you see your career as a business and provide real and tangible guidelines to help you build it.

Just like many businesses start with a single entrepreneur working out of his or her home or garage, your real estate career starts out as a *one-man or one-woman* operation. You are the CEO, CFO, COO and the administrative team and business development team all rolled into one multi-tasking professional. But as you look to grow your business, perhaps even start shadowing more successful agents like I did, incorporating their ideas and systems into your career, or maybe as you bring on a coach to help you develop and refine your lead generating and closing skills, your business will eventually start to grow. At some point, if you are an agent who wants to really build a big business, the workload expands to a point where you start experiencing diminishing returns and the stress and workload start endangering your business. If you are starting to drop balls, or get busy and harried, or lose your mojo and start being less successful in your listing presentations, there is a negative impact on your business and ability to make money.

This is the crucial crossroads that a vast majority of agents struggle with and too often don't successfully navigate. Remember I used the words "dollar productive" activities earlier in the book? This is where rubber meets road. When you reach this point in your career, your focus must become increasingly on being a rainmaker, a prospecting deal closer. It's time to delegate more menial tasks and processes. If you are making photocopies, if you are pushing papers across your desk to different folders, stapling papers and doing other adminis-trative tasks, you are not focused on the real dollar productive activ-ities like prospecting and closing new business. You can pay a high school student minimum wage to do all these necessary (but not truly business-growing) tasks. If you spend half your day chasing all these time-consuming activities, you are working for minimum wage. Think about it conversely; what would you pay a professional who could come in and bring new clients to your business, and get people to sign a listing agreement? The answer is, a lot more than an administrative, minimum-wage earning individual, who is processing business, not generating business.

This is an important and fundamental milestone in your real estate career, and a critical moment where you need to make a radical mind-set adjustment. Your goal is to delegate non-dollar productive activ-ities so you can focus on being a rainmaker. For many, it starts with bringing in part time help to free you up from those menial tasks. For some, letting go and delegating is a real challenge. You "control freaks" out there know who you are. "No one can do it as well as I can," is your mantra. And you know what, this mindset is a liability and it will kill your business. Avoid this trap, if you can. The truth is, no one can do it the same way as you, but with proper documentation and training, they can get it done for you.

So, hopefully, your business starts to grow even more, and that part timer turns into a full-time employee. Then it turns into two full time team members. Perhaps you bring in a buyers agent to free you up from driving buyers all over town. Now you are starting to build a mean, lean real estate selling machine. You are building a team and running a real business! Now you are a going concern, a viable business with great potential.

The most important point you need to know when you are building a team is that you are the leader of that team and **the success or failure of that team rides on your shoulders**. Will you lead a winning team or a dysfunctional team? When you're a team leader it likens itself to the running of a major league sports franchise team like a soccer team. When playing soccer, you need eleven players and one coach. There are eleven players on the field and the coach on the sidelines. At some point in time the coach was one of the players in the game, but he then later became the team's coach, eventually sitting on the sidelines helping to train and lead the team to success. A team is built by its coach: the one who sets the tone, the one who is the impetus for the team's success.

With regards to this scenario I assume the role of the player coach. As a coach for my real estate team, I'm in the game too, only mostly on the sidelines. That's where I have to help various roles shine, because they are critical to the team and the running of the organization. Take the role of the COO, Chief Operating Officer, for example. It may be your office manager, or maybe it's your number two person. I work with them and I then become more of the visionary, setting the mission in place, setting the team goals in place, and then helping and guiding those in their respective roles as I attempt to bring out the very best in every individual team player.

I may not be running the day-to-day practice sessions, but I interact with the COO instructing him/her on the direction we need to be going toward. You're going to have eleven people on the field. You may have other people sitting on the bench that would like to be on the field. Those players who are on the field know that there are players on the bench that desire to be on the field. If you are one of those on the field, you must bring everything you've got or you may not be in the game on a Friday night. If somebody else is hungrier and the coach sees that they may contribute greatly to the overall goal of the team, then that person will be in the game and you may end up on the bench. Therefore, every team player must give his/her very best and fight for their position.

Here's the thing: To get on a team you must first try out. Once you make the team, that's only Phase one. Phase two is you fighting for your position on the team as if somebody else is going to take it away. And believe me, there are other players out there who want to be on that field and want to take your slot. Therefore, there is no room for complacency—not for team players and not for the team leader either. Complacency ultimately is the enemy of a high achiever. You've got to figure out how you start every day at zero. When you go into that practice on a Monday morning, you act as if it is the first practice you've ever been to on that team and you want that coach to notice that you're a player that needs to be on that field in that Friday night game. This is what the coach is looking for, somebody who has that grit, that drive, that ambition, that desire; someone who flat out wants to perform and doesn't come to the game with excuses. This same concept applies in the real estate business as well. And the team leader, the coach, will build a winning team around players who have this mentality of fighting for their position and who won't fall into a state of complacency.

Real estate agents have creative avoidance issues to business development and prospecting. In the book, *Billion Dollar Sales Agent Manifesto*, it says that a billionaire agent, over the span of their career, needs to be prospecting a minimum of one to two or three hours every day. They have no option. The bottom line is that in the real estate business, at the most fundamental level, you're always first a real estate agent. If you're not on a face-to-face appointment with a seller who can list or with a buyer who can buy, then what's next in line on your job description is to spend the rest of that day, however many hours, developing business in an effort to secure a face-to-face appointment. You need to provide yourself an opportunity to help either a seller or a buyer so you can earn a commission. You've got to make something happen! Well, when you are running a team, you have to make sure they are helping you in this quest. They need to be getting you in front of buyers and sellers, they need to contribute to the team's growth and make something happen.

Your #1 Priority: Leadership

As you progress on this journey of personal improvement, or success and growth, and you start assembling the team that is critical to your continued growth and success, it's vitally important to understand that leadership should become your top priority. It sits center stage surrounded by all other components of success—it is what feeds any kind of continued success. Great leaders are not simply born, but they are cultivated through the process of learning and continuously improving themselves. It's the only way they can see growth in others.

In the previous chapter I mentioned the term Kaizen, which means *Change for the Good*. The role of a great leader is to see things not as they are but how they can be—how they can be changed for the good. No matter where a leader is with their team, no matter what level they take a team, a leader should always be looking to see how things could get better. What can make it different? One important thing a leader does when making leadership a priority is that they are always asking questions. To grow in anything in life you must ask better questions. A leader is looking at their team, and they're questioning how could it be better? What do we need to change? What can we do to improve? What can we do to get better, every day, everywhere, everyone? *That's* leadership.

Establish Your Goals

You will see how in this section, many of the fundamentals that we talked about when growing and flourishing as an individual agent also apply when growing a team. You need to have concrete goals and a vision. As a real estate agent, you must determine what it is that you want out of real estate. Ask yourself how you want to lead. For example, do you want to be a single agent operator or do you want to be an agent that has one assistant, or an agent that has three assistants, or an agent that has 15 assistants? What do you want to do?

Somewhere between being a single agent operator and having a larger team of 10 or 15 or 20 people on your team, you should bring in the role of a coach who will ask you what it is that you want, why do you want it, how do you think you're going to get it? Then the coach takes a look at your plan and gets you to do the things that you don't want to do, so you can get what you want. That to me is the core definition of what a coach does. I'll state it again: *"A coach gets you to do the things you don't want to do so you can get what you want."*

If you get a real estate license, you've got to have desire, ambition, and drive. It has to be important enough to you, that you really want to do it. And if it is really important to you, you will do it. On the other hand, if it's really not important to you, then you won't do it, or you won't do it well. What leads in front of all of this, is actually having the drive, the desire, and the ambition. It needs to be so important to you that you are going to accomplish what you set out to do.

If you want to be a superstar you've got to do what the superstars would do. If you want extra, you've got to be willing to take those extra steps. Let me give you an example of an experience I had recently. I went out on a listing for a four or five hundred-thousand-dollar home. I went to meet the seller of the property (in my neck of the woods, that is a higher end property). He was a retired CEO of a bank in Dayton Ohio. When I left our meeting, I realized that his main goal was to investigate the commission. He was shopping for the lowest commission and wanted me to tell him where to price his house and how to position and stage his house to get it sold.

However, his intention was not to hire me, but to use me to bargain and haggle for the lowest price commission possible. A lot of sellers feel like the lowest commission is the best route to take, but it is most times never the best route. At the end of the conversation he was talking about commission, and would say, "Is that your best? Is that your best?" And at some point, I said, "That's my best." And I left. I was upset that I did not get the listing (that's the competitor in me), but I didn't have to grovel or bite the bullet and take a hit on what I am worth in order to get that listing. I had that freedom because my business model, with my branding, advertising, and prospecting, as well as my team who each prospect two hours a day, keeps a steady flow of prospects coming my way. I had the refreshing option to walk away from that business. That should be your business model too.

Here's how I see myself as an example. I take an introspective look at myself and evaluate what are my highest skills, abilities, gifts, and talents. For me, it's being the rainmaker. I am at my best when I am on a face-to-face listing appointment. I'm very effective at developing business through brand image, marketing, and advertising, then going on listings and getting the seller to sign. Those are my greatest skills. At some point in time, that is all, as a team leader, that I do. Therefore, I recognize that I need effective people around me as a part of my team to help run the business that I bring in.

The truth is that I need to prepare to train and lead others who are at least as good or better than me in prospecting and in developing business and marketing opportunities. As the leader, I set the vision that helps others move forward.

How to Lead

I mentioned early about the danger of complacency. A leader should never come in to a task complacent. Complacency allows a mindset of status quo to take place. Your job is to enable change and make sure it's taking place in face of the status quo. The leader is looking to be the change maker to create change, and to challenge. A part of being a change maker is looking to your right and left at those around you who assist you in becoming your best. People want to feel like they're making a contribution; that they're learning something, that they feel appreciated. That's the role of a leader: to acknowledge your team for their efforts.

The leader always looks at the team, and then filters down into the attitudes and actions of each individual. The leader then figures out how to bring out the very best in his or her skills, abilities, gifts, and talents. A great leader is going to show you that you can do more than you thought you could, and that when you accomplish more than what you thought you could, it makes you feel great about yourself and, more importantly, your contribution to the team. A great leader brings out the very best in each individual team player and collectively raises the level of each individual player. In turn, this is a dramatic exponential impact on what the team as a whole is able to accomplish. When your efforts and leadership get your team functioning at its highest level with the team members raising each other's games, there is no greater feeling or accomplishment as a leader. Trust me, it's a rush. It's probably how the manager of the baseball team who has just won the World Series feels.

Every team looks to their leader to take them to the next level of success. Essentially, your team will go as fast or as slow as you move, and as you take them. They're never going to pass you because you're the leader. This is out of respect for their leader. A leader must lead by example—not just talking leading, but actually doing it. There isn't anything that I haven't done in my office, even janitorial, duties. To this day, if I see something on the carpet, I pick it up. A great leader sees what needs to get done and does it, while also instilling those same attributes in their team. That is the culture that a great leader should be creating for his/her team—teaching people how to be self-starters, how to look around and see what needs to get done, and then doing it. They don't linger in excuses and reasons, or creative avoidance. They flat out get it done.

Once when I attended a seminar at the Ritz Carlton, where the level of service excellence is through the roof. I heard a gentleman named Alan Domb apply a powerful credo, or philosophy, to the real estate profession. This philosophy is one of **taking ownership**. As the leader of my real estate team, I've embraced this philosophy. One of the basics within this credo is when an employee or a salesperson in the real estate industry receives a customer complaint they own that complaint. It's his/her responsibility to handle it, and instantly provide a means to appease the client. This type of reaction is required by everyone on the team. The expectation is that the leader and the team reacts to correct a problem immediately and then follows up with a telephone call within 20 or 30 minutes to verify that the problem has been resolved to the customer's satisfaction. We want to do everything possible to never lose a customer or a client. We want them to become our ambassador of good will. We want them spreading only positive experiences about the work that we did for them. An addition to this credo of taking ownership is the standard of uncompromising levels of cleanliness in your specific work area and in the common work area of one's workplace. This is the responsibility of every employee, not just the janitorial service, but everybody. It's a little detail, but very important to the team.

> *A leader is one who knows the way, goes the way, and shows the way.*
> –John C. Maxwell

For example, if you see dirty coffee cups in the kitchenette put them in the dishwasher. Don't take the last roll off the toilet paper, but put a new one on. Be responsible. To me it's critical that I must first be the one to take ownership and do that which I expect my team to do. If the leader doesn't do it, then the team will follow and not take ownership as well.

As real estate agents, my team and I are constantly on 'stage' with every customer and client, and we must always maintain positive eye contact with them. We use words like 'Good morning,' 'Certainly,' 'I'll be happy to,' 'It's my pleasure.' In the real estate industry, I don't just look at what other superstar real estate agents and teams are doing. I look to see what it is that the public expects. They expect *Fedex*-fast, *Disney*-friendly, and an *it's my pleasure* Ritz Carlton attitude. If we're not moving to those levels of what people are experiencing in other industries in the world today, then we're fooling ourselves. A leader also looks outside of his/her own industry looking to see how they're competing on a much larger scale.

I learned a long time ago that the person who keeps the office spotless clean and the person at the front desk are two of the most important people that you can have on your team. The person that is maintaining a stellar work environment is directly affecting the energy of the people on the team because they are a critical player in their area of responsibility in the same way as everyone else on the team. It is necessary to understand that the front desk person is the first contact to the public. It doesn't matter how good my brand image, marketing, advertising, Internet, or social media is. If the person that takes the first client call drops the ball, then I'm dead in the water. All the time, energy, effort, capital that I spent just to get the phone to ring would be, at that moment, non-existent.

My front desk person is a licensed person. Other than myself, I know of no one else who has a licensed real estate agent as a full-time receptionist at the front desk. I want that front person to understand every aspect of the real estate industry because they are a critical key player on the team. I look at real estate companies all across the country and real estate agents all across the country that have weak people as their first point of contact with the public. Inevitably, they end up losing business and they don't even know it. The front desk needs to be a licensed, very skilled, strong, upbeat, happy, personable person who likes people, enjoys interacting with and talking to people and is a service-oriented person. They should be Federal Express fast, have a

Disney friendly attitude and a Ritz Carlton "it's my pleasure" way of being. That's what the public expects.

There are other areas where your team players play a critical role, from the bookkeeper to the chief financial officer to the chief operating officer to the general manager who is handling and accepting contracts, processing the listing, and overseeing the marketing to your courier who's putting up the For Sale sign and measuring the rooms. Or the photographer taking the interior/exterior color photos, or doing the video tours. All of these people represent you and your business. From how they look when they get in front of the public to how they speak, and how they interact with the public, it is all a testament and reflection of you and your leadership.

Ultimately, the team leader is responsible for the result, no different than the coach is ultimately responsible for the result of how their team performs. Greg Andrulis, an MLS (Major League Soccer) coach some years ago for the Columbus Crew, had a stellar team and they were the number one team in major league soccer for the United States of America. He was voted MLS coach of the year. Unfortunately, he subsequently lost some great skilled veteran players to some European countries that were offering the players a higher compensation than what the MLS pays to play here in the United States. Brian McBride was one of those star players. As a result, coach Andrulis lost some of his core players and had to rebuild his team. The next year the team didn't perform at the same level as they did the year before. If you lose some of your core strong players, it will inevitably impact your ability to win future games. Unfortunately, coach Greg Andrulis was gone the following year, even though he was an amazing coach and leader.

To continue the sports metaphor, just like a professional team is a mix of veterans, star franchise players, utility players and rookies, each player has unique needs and requires unique training, coaching and grooming. When you bring on a team player, you need to assess every player's abilities, and more importantly, you look to see what other skills and talents they might have and you leverage those. With every team member, you are sharpening and enhancing their apparent strengths and skills, and you should also be grooming and developing other skills to turn them into the most dollar productive asset you can help them become. I have heard that some agents worry that if they teach and groom a team member too much, they feel that the team member will go off on their own. I disagree with this, if you purposely hold back a team member that does you no good, it doesn't help your team member grow and blossom. You must groom them; help them shine and blossom. Some may leave you, that's true. But many will also stay and want to grow even more. Your responsibility is to keep them challenged, growing, and learning; and keep them incentivized, both mentally and financially. The idea is that you grow them into a higher position and this gives you even more added depth. If a team member has started at the bottom and rises up the ranks, that's a depth of knowledge, which is a great resource. When a team member has done a variety of tasks and assumed a variety of roles, they bring a scope of knowledge that can only help you. Also, if you find that they are also good teachers, they can help you train their replacements.

I have two key team players who have both been with me over 20 years. They each know how to do every process in my business because they've done everything. These two individuals are valuable to my team. One of these team members was brought in as a very green, young gentleman. He is a great example of how you can't judge a book by its cover. He came in with orange hair and tattoos. I saw something in him, so I took a chance on him. He started at the bottom as a courier. As he showed his value, I helped to groom him to each next level. I took him to the store and bought him business clothes, ties, shirts to hide the tattoos, belts, shoes and suits. I helped him grow into earning a six-figure income that he sustained for five years in a row! He is very good at what he does and has helped me grow my business. Like I said, if you take the time to help a team member develop all their skills and talents, it will come back to you tenfold. I took a chance with him and it paid off handsomely!

But as I stated earlier, team members who you've invested time and energy into don't always stay with you as these two star players have. As a team leader, it is imperative that one understands that team members will sometimes leave for a variety of reasons: a job promotion, a new position, an opportunity in real estate, or a family move to a new city. There may even be players that you're going to bring on your team that you may want to let go for various reasons like attitude, how he/she interacts with the team, their productivity, etc. It does not negate the fact that for a leader, a team is necessary for growth and continuous improvement. Life must go on; business must continue.

Part of gaining people's respect in a team environment is understanding that everybody's got to produce in their own individual areas of responsibility and as a team leader it's your job to hold them accountable; to bring them along and bring out the very best in their skills, abilities, gifts, and talents. If they can't perform, then at some point you've got to put them on probation and see if they can step up their desire, their drive, their ambition, and want to accomplish and achieve at a higher level. People need a coach to be able to bring out the very best in them in whatever it is they pursue. If you don't want to build a team and you want to be a single agent operator, then let's use that mindset and my guidance throughout the book to help you become the greatest single agent operator.

As a team leader, you're **not** looking to do real estate the way everybody else does real estate. If you do it the way everyone does, then your inevitable result will be to get what everybody else gets. You must constantly be reinventing and continuously improving how you're going to go about every aspect of the business. Think outside the box with every piece of your marketing, your brand image, your business development, your servicing, and how you interact with people all the time. One just doesn't arrive at success; it takes moving in a direction. This is the C.A.N.I. mindset, the continuous improvement, which means ultimately, you're not going to arrive at a destination—that would be the dreaded complacency! You're relentlessly pushing yourself toward that continuous improvement, but never quite arriving.

The team leader is the player coach; therefore, your number one priority is to lead. With great strength and fortitude, you are now ready for the challenge of assembling your team.

Assemble Your Team

In an effort to successfully grow your real estate business, you can't run it all as a single agent operator. You've got to have help. Getting control of your life and moving toward your dreams means you must learn how to lead a team of people. This involves: learning how to interview people, how to recruit people, train them, and retain them.

Before interviewing, recruiting, and training even begins, you must be prepared. This preparation involves first finding individuals that respect you more than anything else. Many leaders want their team members to like them, and likewise the leader wants to like working alongside their team. However, them liking you is not of utmost importance. If they happen to like you in the end, great! But if they don't respect you first, then they're never going to like you.

As mentioned earlier, at its core, running a real estate team is similar to running a major league sports franchise team. If you've got twenty seats that are available for your team, then you need to find or train and cultivate 20 great players. It is your responsibility to help each team member to access their God given skills, abilities, gifts, and talents as assets for the overall business. This is when a team is really strengthened—when it has players in all twenty positions and no player is a weak link. The team leader then instills an attitude of determination, grit, and success. It is true that your attitude will determine your altitude. You bring yourself to the game. As an athlete in practice, you'll get as much out of that practice as you take into it, and you'll perform in that game to the level that you practiced. It's all about preparing on Monday, Tuesday, Wednesday, Thursday and then at the Friday night game you bring your drive and determination. Leave it all on the field. Never hold back.

Part of gaining people's respect in a team environment is having a full understanding of everyone's individual area of responsibility and setting an expectation for him/her to produce results based on those areas. In turn, as a team leader, it's your job to hold them accountable and to bring out the very best in their skills, abilities, gifts, and talents. There may be instances where you will be tested in your abilities as a leader. This test can reveal itself in the form of a lack of performance by your team members. If this occurs, at some point you will have to put those team members on probation in an effort to challenge them to step up their desire, their drive, and their ambition to achieve at a higher level. If you are committed to running a major league level team, you have to focus on poor performance and help that team member raise their level and perform at your expected level.

Very important, you must be sure everyone on the team knows without a doubt what that expectation is. Spell it out. Well, that player number twenty that is producing at the lowest level is going to get a little bit squirmy because they are struggling to produce at a reasonable level. Set the expectation and monitor their progress. Hold them accountable. If they warrant it and you can see the potential, you may want to coach them up to that level. Just know when it's time to fish or cut bait. Don't let an underperformer with a bad attitude or insufficient skills suck valuable time and energy from you and your mission. Or worse, poison the rest of the team.

One of my trademark beliefs is that every team player ultimately should be funding themselves and every team player is a profit center within the whole organization. That even includes someone on my team like my courier. For example, my courier is responsible for bringing to our team all residential and commercial For-Sale-by-Owner signs. They drive down a street and if they are in a subdivision, they look to the left down that cross street and to the right looking for any For-Sale-by-Owner signs. Because of the actions and contributions of that courier, my team can bring in, on average, one For-Sale-by-Owner a day. That's five a week. That may not sound like much, but it turns out to be 20 a month. That's 250 For-Sale-by-Owners that my courier is out there capturing that we otherwise wouldn't know about. We have opportunities where we'll list some of these For-Sale-by-Owners and then they sign an exclusive right to represent buyer contract with us, and hire us to sell their home and help them find a home. Then we help them find a home and they refer us to someone else—the power of word-of-mouth advertising. That's three transactions from the courier simply letting us know about a FSBO property! That courier and his commitment to finding those signs and bringing them into the team helps our bottom line by tens of thousands of dollars a year!

No matter the size of your team or the number of team members, your goal is to ensure that your team is the best team it can be and that all of you are working in synchronicity. Your goal is to make your team the very best team that ever existed in the real estate industry, whether it's a team of three, ten, or twenty in whatever state and whatever city you live in.

Assembling the best team will sometimes mean you need to brainstorm with *your* personal real estate coach or other top real estate industry people, nationally or internationally, or with CEOs of other companies in other industries and fields. Inspiration is everywhere, and sometimes in an unrelated field or profession. I was involved in an organization called TEC (The Executive Council), now renamed "Vistage," which has different layers of coaching for executives. The way it works is you join a group of other executives like yourself, but they may be in completely different industries or professions or disciplines than you. They might have a CEO of a manufacturing company, the CEO of an electrical company, the CEO of a large restaurant franchise organization, and many more. We would sit in those meetings with these CEO's and discuss the limits, challenges, and problems that we have within our industries and I learned things from their industries that I could bring into mine.

You should always be looking into how you can grow and get better. That's how you will remain viable and relevant. Otherwise, your growth will be stunted and you will plateau if you don't have the mindset of continuous improvement. It can even begin declining. So, you're either going to increase in your productivity, you're going to get stable, or you're going to decline. One of these three things are going to happen to you at any given point in time in your career and honestly, the only way you can continue to surge is to have a mentality and a mindset of continuous improvement. Engage coaches in your life to continually be improving in your performance. That's who we need to become and who we need to be. A leader is either staying stable or increasing and the only way you're going to increase is to have a mentality and a mindset fundamentally rooted in continuous improvement: drive, desire, ambition, and attitude.

You're either going to produce a great result, a mediocre result, or a poor result, but the common denominator in each result produced is *you*. The success of your business is rooted in you. And you will set the tone for your team. Your team will operate their individual areas of responsibility with a mindset of continuous improvement based on the example you set. Trust me, when the entire team is operating under this C.A.N.I. mindset, the results are incredibly powerful!

We can look at a company like Federal Express and learn what they do, what's behind their business model, and what's their unique selling proposition. What makes them better than anybody else in their industry? What makes the Ritz-Carlton, the Four Seasons, some of the best of the best? What makes them different? Go into the Ritz-Carlton and the Four Seasons and look at their physical environment. They're stellar in terms of interior architectural design, furnishings, artwork, cleanliness, how the people are groomed, the uniforms, how they present themselves, and how they interact with the public. If you ask where the men's room is, they don't simply tell you where it is and point you in the direction of the men's room, but they go the extra mile and walk you there. This is excellent service by a team of professionals that are the front and center of the company.

Every team player has a range of influence. And since they are in partnership with me, they are also invested in the success of the business. They may not have the same responsibilities, risk and liabilities that a contractual partner has, but I look at them as associate partners, there to help me grow my business. The combined work ethic of the team will surpass that of an individual acting on his/her own. Once a team is set in place, the level of the performance will inevitably be raised.

You might gain success on your own but you don't need to be the lone ranger. There are great skilled, talented, gifted coaches that have actually done it that can bring you along. Coaches aren't motivated to mentor, train, and challenge their clients based solely on the remuneration they will receive. It's creating a superstar and a superstar's team that is the remuneration for a great coach. I've been doing this for years as a coach for my team. Nothing is more exciting than seeing someone create a better lifestyle for their children and the people who love and care about them the most, and that they love and care about the most. Being a player coach causes you to have an impact on the mentality of who you surround yourself with.

Again, not everybody is going to want to play on a nationally competitive real estate team and maybe as a team leader you don't have the desire to compete at that level. There are grades and levels of teams, and you have to figure out what it is you want to do, and at what level you want you and your team to compete. Much as I did in my wrestling days, I have enjoyed competing at a very high level. More than anything, I enjoy challenging myself to move to the next level but that's always been in me. I always play up. I always surround myself with people that are better than I am. You want to bring people on your team that are going to have different skills, abilities, gifts, and talents than you have because they will bring value to your business and its overall success.

Assembling a successful real estate team does not only entail recognizing and grouping together a set of people who have different skills, abilities, gifts, and talents, but it also entails being the kind of leader who is willing to be tough on their team when necessary. Now, there's going to be varying and controversial philosophies on this topic. Some say you don't need to go into your team player's computers and check the history of where they have been searching and the websites they have been viewing. I believe that as a leader, you do need to check. I once had someone on my team who was sitting at her desk when I came in and she was reading a book while on the clock. I said to her, "Tell me a little bit about your book," so she started telling me about the book and was very excited to discuss the characters and the plot and so on. I responded, "By the way just out of curiosity's sake, are you clocked in or out?" She became embarrassed because she realized she was caught.

That's just an example. I don't like to use it, but it is an example to show that sometimes as a leader you have to be the bad guy. You have a responsibility to raise the level of the productivity of each and every individual on your team. That's the challenging part of being a leader. Now, certainly you want to be relational with all your team players since you work closely with them, getting to know their significant others and their children. It is understandable that you will develop a bond with all your team players, but you also have a responsibility to them because they are looking at you to lead them.

Being Dollar-Productive

As stated earlier, there are nine essential disciplines to having a magnificent real estate practice and a magnificent life in this industry. They are: listing, selling, negotiating and prospecting, interviewing, recruiting, training, retaining and leading the team. For example, you may remember when I mentioned this in the previous chapter that setting up a fifteen-minute listing presentation is a high dollar productive activity.

As a single agent operator, listing, selling, negotiating and prospecting are the four core dollar productive activities. These are at the nucleus of any real estate business.

When leading a large team, your main focus is first on listing, selling, negotiating and prospecting but once you become a team leader, dollar productivity extends into interviewing, recruiting, training, retaining, and leading a team. These are new skills that you will need to acquire. You need to have the skills, abilities, gifts and talents to lead a team and if you don't, then you've got to hire a general manager or a chief operating officer that does have those skills, abilities, gifts, and talents in order for you to grow and sustain a team because you're going to have attrition. You're going to have people join your team and move on to other opportunities, and people who join your team that you may need to let go.

I believe that the nine dollar-productive areas need to be mastered in order to have extraordinary levels of achievement in real estate. The key word here is **mastering**. I believe in continuous improvement, so I believe you can always improve, but you've got to *master* the nine essential elements of dollar productivity. From personal experience, I know that mastering these areas is a challenging process, and very hard to do on your own. You really need to look outside yourself for inspiration, training, and knowledge. Either shadowing other top agents, or even better, finding a great coach to help you elevate your game (and hold you accountable to achieve the success you know you want, but may not be fully disciplined to attain). As a coach to other agents who have sought me out, it is my responsibility to help bring them along in these areas.

It is important to find a coach that's actually doing it and can really relate to the day-to-day challenges and problems that we have today. If they're not doing it, or they used to do it back in the day, or they were dabbling in real estate, they may not have their finger on the pulse of what's happening with the commissions in the industry today or what criteria people are using to select a real estate agent. It's all about the here and now. And in this day and age, the here and now is constantly changing and evolving. As someone who has been in this business for over three decades, it blows my mind how much it has changed, and the change is ongoing and never-ending. It is relentless, and accelerating even! So, how do you do a listing presentation *now*? How do you negotiate *now*? What's more time-effective and efficient *now*? It changes and so the real estate coaches who are not licensed, that are not engaging in real estate or haven't in decades may not be the right player for you. That may be the coach for some, but it may not be the coach for the people who really want to get to the extraordinary levels, that want to get to six-figure incomes or seven-figure incomes, or who want to learn how to get to that level. People often asked me how I got to 5,000 transactions—and now what it is that I am doing to allow me to move towards 8,000 transactions!

Well, that's a long conversation that includes having a work ethic and hard work, perseverance, determination, being willing to make an enormous amount of mistakes and being able to have the strength and the character to get up and brush yourself off and get back in the game. Over the course of my career I have made millions and over the course of my career I have lost millions, and then turned around and made them back. Once you learn how to make that kind of money, if you lose it, then you'll know how to make it back.

Money expands your opportunities and your choices that you otherwise wouldn't have, but it does not create happiness. If you want to talk about happiness, you want to study happiness. Read the Dalai Lama's book, *The Art of Happiness*. It's a great conversation about happiness and where it lives and what it is. It's about learning how to define happiness and what are the elements of happiness. What does that look like? What is that? We all want to be happy but most of us don't spend very much time defining what happiness is to our individual selves. We have a tendency to think that it's all about making more money so we can buy a new car or buy a new this or buy that gadget or this widget. Once you have it, a new house, or an investment, so often you find out that's really not what it was about. Ultimately there's a whole lot that has to do with the relationship that you have with yourself, with your beloved, with your children, with your coworkers, with your friends, and with the people that you do business with.

The idea is that being dollar productive is not solely about money, but also about taking care of yourself. You can't take care of anybody else, not your team players, not the public, not anybody else if you're not taking care of yourself. Here's an analogy: When the airplane's going down and that oxygen mask drops, put it on yourself first and then on the person in the seat beside you. You got to take care of you, because if you don't, nobody else will. Nobody else is going to see to it you're getting the rest, the nutrition, the exercise, the spiritual care, your financial self, your physical self, and your relational self.

Nutrition, rest, sleep, and exercise are the fundamentals, that you must allocate a certain amount of time to. To live a life with an abundance of energy is a wonderful way to live. To live a life with almost no energy is not an empowering way to live a life. To not have the energy to put into life when there's so much energy around us is a shame. We've got to take it in.

Fundamentally, repetition is the mother of learning and I've learned that from my coach. He just keeps driving core key salient points in me that keep getting me back on track. That is one of the most incredible values that a coach brings, they get you back on track, because left alone, we will always get off track. It could be the death of someone close to you. It could be an illness. It could be a team player leaving or it could be a mass exodus of team players. I've experienced that in my career. I've also experienced having 10 buyer agents on my team and then letting them go because they were legends in their own minds but they really weren't producing at a high level.

When you get off track, you can't always get yourself back on track. That's the value of a coach. What you'll pay a coach is so small in comparison to what the coach brings to the party and what they bring to you, both in terms of the quality of your life and how to build and run a team and how to create higher gross commission income and more net bottom-line profits. They're worth their weight in gold — times ten. By the way, I think you should only hire a coach that you pay so much a month, but they also get a percentage of your increase over your previous year's base so the coach has some skin in the game. They're in there with you and want you to really succeed because they have more at stake and a bigger reward if you have a big reward and increase in your income. They're out to help develop you, not just for a month or a year and get paid their monthly fee, but they want to develop a long-term relationship and grow your business to extraordinary levels. A good, committed coach is there with you for the long haul, just as I am in it for the long haul with my clients. I referenced living a life filled with "energy" earlier in this section. I can't tell you how much energy I inject in my life through coaching other agents to higher levels of achievement and accomplishment by sharing the knowledge I have worked so hard to attain. That energy propels me to ever higher success and in my own life. That energy is an important part of me and who I am now, and I can't imagine being without that positive force in my life.

A critical component of developing a team that stays together is a model that is able to be replicated and sustainable for any small business, like a real estate business. Ultimately, as a leader you are the only one responsible. The leader sees things not so much as how they are, but as how they could be or should be, and then begins looking around to decipher how to take his/her team to the next level. As you achieve and move up the ladder, you are constantly reaching for the next rung. As you do, that next rung takes you higher and higher. However, you don't get there alone. The next rung is set in place through the hard work, consistency, and determination of you and your team. Effectively building a team of players within your business rewards you and your team players with a sense of accomplishment, and personal and financial gain. **Never neglect the importance of building a lasting team.**

Strategy 4

Breaking Through Barriers

"You measure the size of the accomplishment by the obstacles you have to overcome to reach your goals."

— Booker T. Washington

In essence, in the preceding pages I've outlined the arc of my career, and told you about what makes me tick. I've shared how I harnessed the good things about my personality (super competitive), and tried to downplay, or minimize, the weaker attributes (my ego and throwing away the "me" wall) to propel me on a fabulous journey to approaching 8,000 transactions. And while it's been a joyous and fabulous journey, there were plenty of failings, obstacles, hurdles, and devastating moments I had to overcome along the way. But that is the essence of success. It's not as much about the triumphs and accomplishments; it's more about how you deal with the adversities, setbacks, and temporary failures that are more instrumental to your march toward victory. Winston Churchill said it best, "Success is not final, failure is not fatal; it is the courage to continue that counts."

For those who are reading the book and are truly motivated to improve and better yourself, and have decided to try *The Phil Herman Method*, those are sage words of wisdom to live by. The one constant you will encounter along the path to your success story is that you will fail—over and over. It's inevitable, just as the ocean waves incessantly pound the beach, life's adversities and challenges will come at you. Over and over. The path to victory and success is always about swimming upstream. The current is rarely in your direction (and when it is, swim as hard as you can to gain as much ground, rather than relaxing and letting the current carry you for a while).

You will hit walls. You will encounter overwhelming odds at times. You will hit barrier after barrier. I can guarantee this will happen to you. It happened to me, over and over. As I said earlier, I've had my head handed to me so many times, but after a while, I also learned how and when to duck. You are defined by how you react to those barriers and setbacks, more than the accomplishments and milestones you hit along the way. C.A.N.I. (Constant And Never-ending Improvement) is all about using these failures, these setbacks, and the obstacles you smack your face on along the way, to sharpen your knife, so you can better cut through them in the future.

A barrier, according to Webster's Dictionary, is a material formation or structure, such as a mountain range or wall that obstructs or impedes and restricts access. In life, we find that the successful ones— the ones willing to color outside the lines and take bold risks—are oftentimes the ones that have had to break through the most barriers. Entrepreneur Richard Branson, founder of Virgin Records, struggled with dyslexia and dropped out of school at age 16. James Earl Jones, the famous actor who has starred on film and stage, and was the iconic voice of the Darth Vader character in Star Wars, suffered from severe stuttering as a child and was very shy and withdrawn. I'm sure the list can go on and on of high achievers in every area, who have not just broken, but kicked down, their life's barriers to reach success.

Barriers can impede and prevent continuous successful growth, yet they can also be the driving force catapulting someone toward their success. Either way, one must work fervently to break through these barriers.

7 Steps to Staying on Top

The strategy for breaking through the barriers entails the seven steps of staying on top and controlling your thinking. First, it is imperative that one understands that growth, success, and maintaining that success is fundamentally all mental and all about **knowing the numbers**. This is step one.

Knowing the numbers, allows one to budget for the challenges, dilemmas, issues, and problems that he/she will inevitably have in this industry. Allow me to give you an example. I know that every time I dial a telephone I make $27.30. Now how do I know that? Upon the urging of my coach, I completed a six-month exercise to find out my average commission for listing calls in a specific category in my real estate business. This category was the expired listings. I logged the number of calls that I made to expired listings, how long it took to make those calls, how many properties I listed, how many sold, and the average commission. I divided that by the number of dials, and the number I came up with was $27.30. Every time I dial the phone, whether the expired seller is there or I get their voice mail, or they hang up on me, I earn an average amount of $27.30.

Your attitude will determine your altitude.

By doing this exercise for six months and turning those daily accountability sheets into my coach, I learned a great deal about my commission on listing calls, and how much my time was really worth. The telephone became a propellant. Knowing those numbers was a propellant for me to get on the phone because I'd essentially be making $1,000.00 an hour. Using the predictive dialer, I knew how many calls I could make in an hour because the computer dials the phone for me. The computer leaves the pre-recorded voice mail messages for me. On the other hand, the agent that doesn't know their numbers is not going to see the telephone as the same propellant that it is for me to get on it every day.

The second step in breaking down barriers is your **attitude**. I've seen people that have extraordinary skills, abilities, gifts and talents, but had a poor attitude. Having a poor attitude will ultimately lead to self-sabotage. Not having the proper mindset and not mastering the mental side of the game can hold us back. This is a critical, essential part to achieving at high levels whether you're an athlete, a parent, a friend, a coworker, a CEO, or a team leader. One's attitude is directly connected to one's mental side. Therefore, controlling the internal conversation that is fired at us point blank all day long, every day is going to have a significant impact on your level of achievement and somewhat dependent on how you're going to manage your attitude. You *can* do something about attitude. If you have a bad attitude, you've coached yourself into being a whiner, a complainer, and just a negative kind of person. Well you can turn that around and let it go; you don't have to live with that forever.

To excel at high levels, among many things, one must maintain an attitude of success. If this is you, and your business is excelling at really high levels, then I would say you should pat yourself on the back. This means that you've learned the value of a great attitude, you've controlled the mental side of the game. You have effectively broken through another barrier. One after another after another. So how were you able to do this? Your goals and your dreams are important to you, and that's why you were able to do, be, and have what it was that you wanted in life. If you're somebody that is at the bottom of the barrel and you're scraping, it doesn't mean that you have to stay there. It will begin with you first getting out from the bottom of the barrel and learning how to master that internal conversation that you have with yourself every day, which I believe is the most important conversation that we have with ourselves. You know, the conversation where you tell yourself that you're not good enough, smart enough, or courageous enough to do something great or run a successful business. Listening to this negative internal voice will undoubtedly keep you at the bottom of that barrel while others reach out of it and soar past it. However, changing your attitude will also change the internal conversation you have with yourself.

It is important to figure out how to get leverage on yourself to do the things that you know will help you get what you want. This is a key benefit to hiring a coach. A coach is going to help you do what you don't want to do so you can get what you want through an account-ability relationship and process. It's really all mental.

Controlling the mental side of the game for me starts before I put my feet on the floor when I get out of bed in the morning. I read a book once called *The Greatest Salesman in the World* by Og Mandino. Within the contents of that book there are 10 scrolls. One of those scrolls read:

"Today I will begin a new life. I will greet this day with love in my heart. I will persist until I succeed. I will multiply my value 100 fold. 'I will multiply my value 100 fold' is a very artistic way of saying that you are going to prospect in the real estate business world consistently on a daily basis to get better and better."

I chant these words before I get out of bed every morning: *Every day in every way I am getting better, better and better.* It's sort of a cleansing before I begin my day. There are times when maybe the day before doesn't go quite as well as you may have thought. Life happens, but how will you choose to deal with it? From death to divorce, to sickness and illness, to sadness with your loved ones... Life shows up and happens. The purpose in chanting those words every day is to clear my mind before I put my feet on the floor, to begin with a fundamental self-talk. Today I begin a new life so I'm starting at zero. Every day in every way I'm getting better, better, and better. I'm forgiving of myself for all the errors and mistakes, things I shouldn't have said or should have said, or didn't apologize for or should have apologized for. I've got to lift myself up. In life and in success, self-talk is absolutely critical. We're constantly faced with that conversation that goes on inside of every one of us. You may not be fully aware of this internal monologue you are having. Maybe it's fallen to the background and you don't pay attention to it. Everyone has it. If you pay attention to it, you can direct it in a positive way before it controls you in a negative way.

Today, choose to begin a new life where you will say, "I will greet this day with love in my heart. I will persist until I succeed. Persistence and determination can be your catalysts to success. When I persist until I succeed, that is what defines success for me. When I control my attitude, I can, do, be, and have anything that I want in life—if it's important enough to me."

So, which conversation are you going to pay attention to? When you're setting out your goals and plans, you must spend a lot of time contemplating how important they are to you. If your goals and plans are not really important to you, you won't do what it takes, which are the action steps that you need to take to implement massive action on the plan that you ultimately create. Think about what's important to you in life. Think about whether you are on or off track. Asking yourself these types of questions and contemplating your life is all a part of breaking through barriers and controlling your attitude.

It's important to consider the "why" behind your goals, just as much as the "how." A goal becomes so much more powerful if you remember the "why" behind the reason for attaining it. For instance, if your goal is to increase your production from 10 homes a year to 15 homes, what does that extra income represent? A big vacation? Buying an investment property? College Tuition for your kid? See, if you focus on five more sales, it's one thing, but if you can see the end result of those five extra sales, you have more motivation.

I think ultimately the fundamental key is your self-image. Who are you going to be in the face of whatever obstacle does show up in life? That's a question to meditate on. Whether it is rejection, illness, or the loss of a loved one; Whether it is business failure or financial loss. Ultimately, it is about you and your attitude. Who are you going to be in the face of whatever negative circumstance that shows up? You must figure out how to brush yourself off and get back in the game every day so that every day in every way you are getting better and better. Your self-talk before you put your feet on the floor in the morning should be focused and empowering.

Alongside empowering and focused, your self-talk should also be very forgiving. **Forgiveness** is the third step to staying on top. The more you learn to forgive yourself, the more effective you will be at forgiving others. The less you're able to forgive yourself, the harder you are on yourself, consequently the harder you'll be on all the people that are around you. The forgiveness aspect is huge, because when we make mistakes, going in our blind spot, we tend to beat ourselves up and we don't forgive ourselves. We spend mental energy at the start, beating ourselves up and not forgiving ourselves, versus being like a Tiger Woods with a bad shot. He forgets it, forgives himself, and moves on.

So much of professional sports is mental. When a major-league pitcher throws a pitch and the batter hits a home run, he has to keep his composure and not let it get to him. Or else, the next pitch may be hit out of the park. You see it all the time, the pitcher makes a mistake, and then just slides into one mistake after another until the manager pulls him out of the game. You'll see the pitcher's infielders try to help him regain his focus sometimes. It's important to forgive, move on, and refocus.

That's what you have to do. You've got to know your blind spot. Many times we learn our blind spot through failure.

It's very difficult when we make a mistake. Oftentimes, we have a tendency to beat ourselves up over the mistake. Instead, when you make a mistake, a new trigger could be rather than dwelling on the negativity of the mistake that you made, ask yourself a better question: Having made that mistake, what can I learn from it? What can I do better? How can I use that as a leverage to be a springboard for much higher levels of achievement in whatever it is that I'm trying to do? **Mistakes, ultimately, can be our greatest teachers.** I have a whole lot more to teach any real estate agent in the area of the mistakes than in the successes that I've achieved. It's what I did after committing those mistakes that defines me more than my successes, in my opinion.

Meditating can be an effective tool to forgiving ourselves, and focusing on the positive. At one time in my life I was a really angry young guy and I had to learn that my anger never made me any money. It cost me more money than I could ever begin to imagine. I started reframing how I was going to look at my anger. Thich Nhat Hanh, the author of a book called *Anger: Wisdom for Cooling the Flames*, says, "When your anger shows up, go to it like it is a crying baby." Basically, in doing that you are attempting to find out what is wrong and effectively finding a way to make it better...like a baby. Does it need to burp? Is its diaper wet? You go to your anger like a crying baby and try to figure out what it is, tenderly. What I also found out was that oftentimes anger is a natural response we have to protect ourselves from hurt. The anger is protecting some kind of pain that's within that little boy or that little girl that's inside of us.

You go to the pain to figure out what that is. It's the quickest way to get yourself out of an anger state. You can beat yourself up forever over the mistakes that you've made in life, or you can choose to listen to another conversation within yourself, forgive yourself, and then learn from those mistakes. What could I have done better? How is this going to leverage me to new levels, new heights of achievement, and accomplishment or happiness?

Overcoming fears and taking action are our next two steps—steps four and five. In order to be a super achiever, you've got to expect that you would have some fears. However, you must also learn to overcome them. I once heard Tony Robbins say that the antidote to fear is action. That's where the power lives. The power is action. These words cannot be more true!

That's it—that's the key to personal power. If what Tony is saying is true, if action is the key to personal power, then to take action on a consistent basis, to me, is the antidote to fear. Fear immobilizes us and stops us from taking action. So fighting that paralysis, by taking action, is the key to personal power.

When one finds oneself in the face of fear, oftentimes the immediate response is to freeze and become immobilized. We don't act. However, it is always better to take an action than to take no action at all. If you take an action and it's the wrong action, you can then take a new action to correct the wrong action. To do nothing will essentially produce nothing. The way I see it is that you can think it through, you think about what the right course of action is, and then you act on it. For example, in a business, you might want to brainstorm with your board of directors. I have a mastermind group around me that I can call and say, "Here's the challenge or dilemma that I'm having. Have you ever experienced that yourself? What action do you think I should take?"

Ultimately, whatever situation you face in life or in business, you will be forced to look at the person in the mirror and decide who you're going to be in the face of it and what action step you're going to take in the face of it. Overcoming fears in order to have forward movement towards happiness means that you must learn how to take action in the face of fear. In most situations, fear is going to be present. It's a part of the dynamic of being human. We're going to be faced with fears and we've got to have a little bit of faith in ourselves that we can overcome this, whatever it may be. Whether it's obesity, whether it's a negative attitude, or whether it's creative avoidance to not get on the phone and prospect … **do not** sabotage yourself out of fear.

I can't emphasize enough the benefits of working with scripts and dialogues in your real estate career. Agents often don't achieve success because prospecting on the phone or face-to-face can be a fearful thing to do. They come up with creative avoidance out of their fear to not do it. Forcing yourself to learn scripts and dialogues to overcome the fear of getting on the phone to prospect is basically a necessary evil for real estate agents. Oftentimes I find the reason real estate agents don't prospect is because they don't know what to say, so they don't get on the phone. If people don't know what to say, they're not going to get on the phone. The scripts and dialogues are really not difficult to learn; it's just about being conversational.

Scripts and dialogues are all rooted in three fundamental processes: **Who are you? Why are you calling? What do you want?** When you call a prospective client, you must understand their mindset and think in terms of the receiver of the call. They want to know who are you. Who is calling them. They also want to know, should I stay on the phone with you and what's in it for that potential client to stay on the phone with you? Whether you're calling your sphere of influence, your past clients, For-Sale-by-Owners, just listed, just sold, your follow-ups, a geographical farm or renters for first-time buyers, it doesn't make any difference. If you understand that those three fundamental parts are what make up a script and dialogue and make it conversational, you will bring in those clients you need.

You've got to address these fundamental processes as a baseline right out of the chute. You're calling them to tell them who you are and why you're calling. I give them my 15-second elevator commercial, which gives them a reason to stay on the phone with me or to perhaps want to meet with me and know a little bit more about what I might be able to do for them. Then, I extend an invitation for them to come into the office to meet with me.

Master these scripts and dialogs and you will want to get on the phone and take action because you know that it works. Once you start experiencing the wins from the high-impact prospecting on the phone, then it takes on a life of its own. Let's go over an example of a script again:

"Hi, my name is Phil Herman. I'm the broker/owner at RE/MAX Real Estate Specialists. Sir, just very briefly, the reason I called is that I noticed your listing might have expired. Was that correct or did you sell it? Just out of curiosity's sake, why were you selling? Are you staying local or moving out of the area? If you were to move, where would you move next? When would

that be? Who else do you know that's thinking about buying or selling any residential or commercial real estate that I might be able to help?"

"Sir, we haven't met, but allow me just give you my 15-second elevator commercial. I own the company. I've been doing this full-time for over 30 years. Individually, I've done over 7,000 transactions. Nobody in our region's ever done 2,000 or 3,000 transactions, as far as I know. The average agent, nationally, only does about five home sales a year, so 7,000 is a bundle. I've outsold a field of 3,000 agents 27 years straight. I was ranked in the Top 100 Nationally out of about 1 million real estate agents 3 years in a row by Realtor® Magazine. The only reason I tell you that is so you know I'm not new; I'm not part-time and I know I can help you. At least I'm in the best position to get you and your family the most amount of money in a reasonable amount of time with the fewest problems possible. I know that's what you want. Isn't it?"

"There probably wouldn't be anything that would come up on your home or on your property, sir, that I haven't had to deal with maybe 1,000 times before, somewhere in my past. So you're in good hands. I was wondering, why don't we set up a time for you to come into the office? That would give us a chance to get acquainted, for me to go over your needs, see if I think I can help you with your needs, but also for you to see if you feel like I'm the kind of realtor you'd like to hire to go to work for you. When would be a convenient time for you to come into the office?"

The script is on an expired listing. What I did was: I called and I introduced myself to him and told them who I was and why I was calling. I gave them a reason, my 15-minute elevator commercial, to stay on the phone and to listen. Then, through that, I gave them a compelling reason to perhaps want to meet with me and then I extended the invitation. The reason real estate agents, in my opinion, don't get on the phone and do high-impact prospecting is because they haven't "done the numbers" like I have (remember my $27.30 per call calculation?). They haven't brought in $1,000 or $10,000 or hundreds of thousands of dollars from doing high-impact prospecting. I brought into my world millions of gross commission income, millions plural, from doing high-impact prospecting.

As a matter of fact, it's been at the core of my feat of approaching nearly 8,000 transactions and nearly a billion dollars in sales volume. I'm very passionate about it. For me, it's a ritual. It's something that I do every day because I've overcome the fear aspect of high-impact prospecting, of getting on the phone and calling a stranger and asking if they would consider doing business with me. Have you ever noticed that when you got your real estate license your phone never rang? People didn't just all of a sudden decide, "Gee, I heard Phil Herman got his real estate license. Let's call him." It doesn't work that way. You've got to get on the phone and extend the invitation, give them a reason to want to meet with you. Reach out to them.

Do the thing you fear and the death of fear is certain. An agent can get over their fear by picking up the phone, and calling the list of 20 or 30 expired or For-Sale-by-Owners in front of them as long as they have an adequate script. If they would just get over the fear, make the phone call and spend an hour or two doing that, they would start conquering that fear. And as you learned, every time they pick up the phone they're going to make 20 bucks. Pretty soon, that agent will get motivated to pick up the phone and get better at their script. And if you pursue this, you're going to find that you get a listing. It all happens because of the action, going back to what Tony Robbins said. Personal power is the ability to take action. Don't get stagnant. Don't allow fear to put you in prison—so break out of prison by taking action!

You're either going to listen to the fear conversation that's going on inside you or you're going to listen to the empowering, taking action side of the conversation that's going on inside you. Depending on which one you give the most listening to, it'll impact whether you do high impact prospecting, or whether you do build a personal brand image and hire somebody to help you with good image marketing, branding, and advertising. Whether you'll build a team or not build a team, learn the scripts and dialogues to overcome objections and have good presentation skills. **Put systems in place: Lead a team, recruit, train, retain, list, sell, negotiate and prospect.** So, are you going to listen to fear and allow it to immobilize you and hold you back? Or are you going to listen to action, which I believe is the antidote to fear.

Now, let's continue on to the sixth step for staying on top and breaking barriers: **Shadow others**. Shadowing is a way to learn how to overcome fears and take action by seeing it in action from someone else. This is done by visiting them and taking the time to *shadow* their business. There is great value in shadowing another real estate agent, especially in helping to break through barriers and see new ways of doing things. Shadowing was the most important process that I implemented in my career, and it was birthed out of fear.

I was doing okay, but I could see those around me were doing so much better. Then, I read a book, and most of us are familiar with it. It's called *Think and Grow Rich*, by Napoleon Hill. Back in the day, he shadowed the movers and shakers of our country to figure out what were the common denominators in what they were doing that we're allowing them to have high levels of achievement and success. He set out on a journey to do that and wrote one of the most renowned books ever written in *Think and Grow Rich*. It's been said that it's been responsible for creating more millionaires than any other book, only second to the Bible.

> *"The key to personal power is the ability to take action on a consistent basis."*
> —Tony Robbins

So, I set out on my own shadowing journey. As I referenced earlier, I once got invited, some time ago, to the Realtors® National Marketing Institute of the National Association of Realtors. They pulled together about 50 of the top agents at the time. I was one of those agents. The goal was to do mastermind sessions and brainstorming. Nobody was from the same state. There was a free flow of information. I decided that if I learned so much from this short mastermind session, I wanted to shadow these top agents and learn even more. I set out on a mission to shadow some pretty extraordinary agents at the time, from Karen Bernardi to Allan Domb to Ron Rush to Bob Bohlen, just to name a few. I shadowed 30 to 40 agents in four years. I knew I had to do this to break through my personal and professional barriers. I understood that seeing it done by another agent would be the best way to learn what actions to take, and I would have concrete proof that this action would work.

I spent anywhere from three to five days shadowing each one of them. Going to their cities, to their offices, looking at their business models, and their operating systems. And also, interviewing their team players. All of this was in an effort to try to understand how they brought business in the door, what kind of high impact prospecting they did, and what kind of marketing image management. How did they build their teams? What kind of people did they surround themselves with? What kind of scripts and dialogues did they use? What kind of systems did they have in place? How did they overcome objections? What were their listing presentations like? What were their buyer presentations like? How did they work as a team? How well did they work? What were the characteristics of the team players? What was each team player doing? How did they lead? What were the key common denominators in these extraordinary great agents that were leading magnificent teams and doing enormous amounts of business, providing high levels of consistent quality service to the public, serving one another? These were all critical questions to ask and find answers to.

This was a massive task that I took on for four years. It was a lot of airplane rides, a lot of hotels, and a lot of notes. In fact, I'm still shadowing Bob, making it my eighth time shadowing him. He's a really great, magnificent, powerful, and high level achieving agent. Shadowing an agent like him only once is not enough. You get an overview, a good overview, of what they do and how they do it. I've shadowed top agents multiple times, not just once, so I could dig a little bit deeper.

Consequently, I have agents all over the country that now come and shadow me here in the Midwest. It's an interesting process. I tell them, "This is how much it costs for you to shadow me for a day. At the end of the day, if you don't feel like you got that kind of value, I'll give your check back to you." The great part is that I've never had to give anybody a check back. I ask them to write down a hundred questions before they come, and email me that list of questions, and promise them that I'll cover all 100 questions. I then have a curriculum that I cover with them, including those disciplines that I was referring to before, from high impact prospecting to brand image marketing management, to building a team, the quality of the team players, learning the scripts and dialogues, having systems in place, overcoming objections, learning good presentation skills, learning how to lead, and knowing how to service the public and your team. I make sure that I cover the core disciplines within our industry.

You can learn more from shadowing a high level, high achieving agent, than you can learn in a year of coaching by phone. That's how powerful I believe shadowing is, and why I still do it today. Again, I've been shadowing top agents for decades. This isn't something new to me. Craig Proctor was an agent that I shadowed in Toronto, Canada. He was the leading RE/MAX agent in the world, multiple years in a row. Craig and I became very good friends. As a matter of fact, he is the agent I mentioned previously when we launched a marketing campaign together one night at about 11 o'clock at night in his office with him and his marketing associate. That campaign is something I still use to this day and it has brought me so much revenue from Expireds and For-Sale-By-Owners. Shadowing is something that you absolutely want to put into your business plan to help you break through barriers. It will help you control your thinking. These other top agents that I shadowed are the best examples because they have mastered these things already: controlling their thinking, looking over the blind spots, and overcoming their fears.

Shadowing is an element of your quest for continuous improvement. Included in this continuous improvement is developing a habit of listening. For example, I set out on a task to listen to a thousand TED talks. Then there is reading. Make an effort to set a goal to read a certain number of books per year. Attend seminars. I've already paid $10,000 to his organization and I plan to attend Tony Robbins' Business Mastery and Immersion Seminar for a week. Even as successful as I have become, I still hire a marketing coach and a real estate coach to hold my feet to the fire, keep me on track, and hold me accountable. This coach will help me achieve my goals and see to it that I'm actually implementing a business plan.

Continuous improvement involves being forgiving of myself, because if I make a mistake, I try to figure out, well, what could I have done better, what can I learn from that mistake, instead of beating myself up. It's just about getting better. The concept of continuous improvement has been with me since before real estate. It was with me as a young, high school athlete. It was with me as a college wrestler. It's always been in my mentality. As an athlete, I was always putting myself in situations with players that were much better, older, and more skilled than I was. I wanted to compete and train with the college athletes when I was in high school. I was always looking for somebody that was better than me to raise my game.

So, this was a natural ebb and flow for me when it came to real estate. I believe that continuous improvement is in my DNA, and then when I learned the word, "Kaizen," the Japanese business life philosophy, it became a study for me. Learning how to apply it into the real estate sales environment has been a fundamental philosophy of achievement. Forward movement towards happiness.

The last step in breaking through barriers is to **hire a marketing company**. (This step will inevitably be followed by the hiring of a coach.) Hiring a marketing company helps you break through a barrier and helps your company or business reach new heights. Do not take the approach of For-Sale-by-Owner on your marketing, on your image, or on your brand. That would be one of the biggest mistakes I think a real estate agent could make. Thinking that they can handle their own brand image, and marketing is not the way to go. Who knows more about selling a home, the home owner looking to save money by selling themselves or the agent who has years of experience? We know that studies show the majority of FSBOs end up listing the home with an agent in the end, so they lose time, money, and momentum by trying to go it alone. Over 25 years ago, I hired a company named Hobbs Herder Advertising that specializes in the real estate out of Southern California, because I knew how important branding was, and that it wasn't my particular skill, ability, gift, or talent. I did not have a degree in marketing, so I wanted to put somebody that knew way more about it than me in charge of that part of my business. I knew how important it would be.

It's sort of like this: My photo is on my sign and on all my marketing materials because my photo is really my logo. There are nearly 3,000 agents in the Dayton and Northern Cincinnati market, which is where I specialize. So, when it comes to marketing and branding myself, one of the first questions I ask myself is, "How am I going to get anybody to ever pick me?" From the beginning, I was always about marketing me, the individual, and not the company. So many agents make the mistake of going it alone with their marketing, but instead, they end up marketing the company because that's what they think you are supposed to do.

You are the product. You are the brand. Your story is what will sell, not the company's story. Sure the company is an important validation for the consumer, that's where your company's marketing and branding expenditures and campaigns will help you. But you are the focus, backed by the resources of your company, and not the other way around. Companies that I have worked with have been very traditional companies that had somewhat of an old-fashioned view towards how real estate would be done. They were really not the innovator-creators of new techniques and new ways of doing business, but they were very successful companies and doing the lion's share of the transactions within the board of Realtors®. But they were not really cutting-edge from what I had learned and exposed myself to from shadowing 30 or 40 of the top agents multiple times all across the country.

You must remember that your marketing goes out in the community before you ever pick up that phone. The key is to look at marketing as reverse-prospecting, branding, and how it helps your script and dialog.

Early on in my career, I decided that I would not attempt the For-Sale-by-Owner approach to marketing and branding. Now, what I mean by the For-Sale-by-Owner approach is that someone who is selling their home as For-Sale-by-Owner thinks they know more about the real estate industry than anyone else. Oftentimes, For-Sale-by-Owners get themselves in trouble or sell their properties below what they could have sold for had they exposed it to a larger pool of buyers through a professional real estate agent. Maybe a real estate agent can't show the home as well as the homeowner can, because the homeowner lives there, but the real estate professional is certainly going to expose that house to a larger pool of buyers that the owner does not have access to. The real estate agent can also offer services that the For-Sale-by-Owner seller doesn't offer, and, in my case, I've successfully negotiated 7,000 transactions as a third-party negotiator.

I suggest to real estate agents all over the world to not go For-Sale-by-Owner on their brand, or their image. You want somebody to professionally handle you and coach you. When you are on the inside and so close to it, it can be hard to notice the little details. You're standing in your shadow, where you think you might know. It's good to have an expert, an absolute expert, in that arena to give you some input and some guidance. It is one of the most important tools that you're ever going to have working for you as you move forward into your career.

Here's a specific example of what I mean. A brand-new agent, or an agent that doesn't do very much real estate, gets on the phone to call an expired listing, and says, "Hi, my name is Billy Bob, and I'm with ABC Realty." That expired seller, if they've never heard of the name

ABC Realty or the real estate agent Billy Bob, will not receive that agent very well.

On the other hand, what I've tried to do for over 30 years in my career is build a brand and an image so that when the consumer thought of real estate in Dayton, Ohio, they would think of Phil Herman. The way they would think of Phil Herman would be as the top real estate agent in the region, nobody gets the results that he does; he provides the public with the best and the highest quality of consistent service, and he knows what he's doing. In addition, he's excellent at marketing, he's a great negotiator, and we want to interview with him. When I call them, they know my name and they know my company and therefore, they are receptive to me. That has been achieved through a very strategic and consistent branding and marketing campaign.

The interesting thing is that in the early days, I had to invest a larger percentage of my income back into my branding and marketing. Ironically, when you are starting out and you need the income from your work most, that's when you need to invest more of your income back into growing your business. What I've found over the years is that agents don't tend to look at their work as a business. If you were to open a sandwich shop, you wouldn't open your doors for business and hope that people walk in, would you? You need to advertise and get people in the door to start talking about your business, to come back again, and hopefully, they will start recommending your establishment to their friends. Savvy business owners would not dare open a business without an advertising budget. It's part of the plan. I will tell you that your real estate career is no different. You have to invest in growing your business. If you can't afford a direct mail campaign, you need to door knock and/or network with lots of people to get the word out.

Ironically, the more successful your business becomes and grows, the less of a percentage of your income has to go into marketing. Now, that I am making more money, it's a lower percentage that I need to keep and maintain my branding, name recognition, and marketing reach. Like most agents, I started out doing direct mail to a concentrated farm area. Over the years, as I grew my business, my marketing moved more toward "mass" media, like newspaper ads, billboards, television commercials versus concentrated mailing or farming to a specific area. It's important to know that you can't coast or stop your branding and marketing. Otherwise, you'll experience diminishing returns, and possibly let another agent pass you.

As an agent who has created a very powerful brand through my marketing and advertising, I have a very distinctive advantage over the other 2,000 to 3,000 real estate agents in the region because in the consumers' minds they see me as being the leader. Being the leader is *owning* that position in the mind of a consumer, and it's a powerful position in the real estate industry, or in any industry. That comes from a book written decades ago by Al Ries and Jack Trout called *Positioning*. In that book, one of the chapters states that being number one in a category is a very powerful position to hold. This was one of the goals I set out to do. It became part of my Kaizen, if you will, to continually improve my brand image, my marketing, and my advertising, so I could own that number one position in the mind of the consumer.

Real estate agents, I suggest that you hire a professional marketing company to coach you and guide you into that critical area of your business. You must maintain a good brand and powerful marketing and advertising materials through the internet and social media, internet marketing and advertising, as well as all the traditional means from TV to billboard to direct mail to print advertising. I believe that having a mix of both the old and the new is the most powerful way to target your audience and create a lasting brand.

High-impact prospecting is where you are calling clients, or potential clients, and inviting them to do business with you. Having a good brand and good image, marketing and advertising in place for yourself, where the public is calling and asking you if you'll come out and handle their real estate needs, is **reverse prospecting**. When you do both aggressively, as I have, it is a powerful force to be reckoned with. This is what hiring an effective marketing company does for you.

I believe marketing and high-impact prospecting go hand-in-glove. You don't do one or the other, you do both, and you do both on a consistent basis throughout your entire career. You should never, ever stop either one of them. You're always trying to figure out how to strengthen your business—your brand—to make it better, more effective, and more efficient. Marketing, brand image management, advertising, social media, internet marketing and advertising, are the tools you need to use to continuously improve.

But wait, there's more. In order for these steps to remain intact and sustainable, you will need to hire a coach to keep you on track.

The #1 Key to Success

Accountability is where the rubber meets the road to make sure you are being effective every day. The number one key to success is daily accountability, because no one gets there alone. This is the invaluable role of a personal coach in business. If I had not hired Bob as my business coach, I would not be where I am today. It's one thing to learn how to be successful from a book, but it's another thing to talk to a coach every Monday who is directly challenging you on your goals for achieving success.

Tony Robbins, for example, influenced me differently than Bob did. Greg Herder, in marketing and advertising, influenced me differently than Tony did, and differently than Bob did. This was all by design. Bob is a consummate business mind. He is one of the most magnificent—genius—prodigy business minds that I've ever been around. He represents one key person on a *personal board of directors*, you might say, that I want to have in place. Greg Herder had a strength, ability, gift, and talent that I didn't have that I needed in order for me to grow. Bob was a phenomenal business coach, and Greg was a magnificent marketing coach. And Tony Robbins got me to think differently and challenge myself. He taught me to learn how to ask myself better questions about life and about my business. That's a different kind of coaching.

I haven't just had one coach; I've had multiple coaches. Without question, if you're in the real estate industry, you will create a significant advantage and leverage yourself beyond your wildest imagination when you hire a coach whose fundamental basic job description is to help get you to do what you **don't** want to do, so you can get what you want. That is their focus. A great coach will help you do what you don't want to do, so you can get what you want. And the things that you don't want to do are oftentimes the things that are sabotaging your own success. A great coach is going to hold your feet to the fire and keep you on track. Nobody gets there alone. Nobody.

So, since you don't get to that successful place alone, take action. Utilize your team and the marketing coach/company you've hired for your company. Then, hire a great business coach, someone who understands the real estate business and has actually done it.

There are many, many coaches to choose from in the marketplace. There are new real estate coaches entering the arena every day. In my opinion, there are good coaches, there are great coaches, and even some mediocre coaches, all vying for your hard-earned dollar. I understand that there are even real estate coaches who have never sold real estate in their life, or they have left the game so long ago, they are out of touch with the reality you have to face every day.

I'm suggesting that you choose a coach that has done it, and preferably, is actually doing it now. My coach, Bob Bohlen still sells real estate. I wouldn't have it any other way, my coach has to be in the game, just like I am.

Experience speaks volumes. Make this part of your criteria when you are hiring a coach. Just as you used criteria when selecting a marketing person. You knew beforehand that your marketing coach had to have a degree in marketing, and was good at marketing themselves and their own company. You looked at their marketing efforts for other agents. So goes it with a coach. You want to know that the real estate coach you're thinking of hiring has actually done something in the field; that they've achieved individually, at a high level, in residential real estate sales over a long, sustained period of time.

When I say to you that I've done close to 8,000 transactions and a billion dollars in real estate sales, I don't want you to view that as me being cocky, conceited, or arrogant. I want you to hear that there's a confidence that comes with my record. I've worked with a team, and helped mentor the contributions that they make. I have not done it alone. I've done it with coaches helping me along the way. I've done it with great team players. Nobody gets up there alone and without help. That's why I opened my book with that thought that life is all about relying on other people if you want to reach peak performance, whether you are an athlete or a real estate agent.

There are so many aspects of real estate and achieving at high levels. It can be a daunting task. Overwhelming. That fear can immobilize you from challenging it, and moving into it and growing. Taking massive action. Build a great board of directors around yourself, as I'm suggesting. Have somebody that helps you in the area of your spirituality. Look at some areas that you want to grow in your life: family or marriage.

I bring this up because I know that the divorce rate is at fifty percent and growing. Building a business and a career requires a lot of focus, time, and resources, both mental and financial. If you are not careful, it can put a strain on your relationships. As you *bake your cake* that is your career, as you invest your heart and soul into a magnificent real estate business, if you find yourself struggling in this area, that's the one powerful source for you to look to. Take the time to find balance as you grow your magnificent real estate business, and not lose sight of the important things in life.

Breaking through barriers ... Learning how to master the mental side of the game ... Understanding that it's all about numbers ... Creating a magnificent board of directors around you, and having a great marketing coach so you don't go for sale-by-owner in your marketing and advertising ... Shadowing top agents. These things are the noble activities, the "massive action" we are talking about. I get inspired when agents choose to take massive action and come out to shadow me. I've had so many agents come to the Midwest, Dayton and Northern Cincinnati, to see what I do and how I do it. To see me on a listing presentation, live and in the moment, or negotiating a contract. To see the quality of the team players that I've brought in, what they do, how effective and efficiently they work together, and the energy they put out. They also see how they put up monthly goals, how we gauge performance, and what key indicators we watch and focus on.

If you recall me mentioning previously, one month, my team set out to set up a hundred appointments in a thirty-day period. Then there was a reward system in place where I took them all to dinner and gave them all a thousand dollars that they have to go spend in two hours, and then come back for dessert and share what they bought themselves. Just a fun evening together. We set a high bar or goal. The reward has to be special and something unique to generate a hundred appointments in a thirty-day period. Grand goals need to be celebrated in a grand way, otherwise your team grows weary and cynical.

It's all about learning to control your thinking, and also knowing your blind spots. Whatever you want in life — you can do, be, and have whatever it is that you want if it is important enough to you. Get your mind and body into the game, every day, every play. Prior to a listing, give yourself focus prompters. It's show time before you go into a listing, so get the clutter out of your mind. That is why this chapter on breaking through barriers, the mental side of the game, is absolutely essential. It's critical. If it sounds like I'm on a rant, it's because I am. This is so important people. If you admire all the champions of the world, the Michael Jordans, the Kobe Bryants, the Serena Williams, the Mia Hamms and the Tiger Woods of the world, then you are admiring exactly this mindset. Their level of focus and passion for excelling is exactly why they are champions. You can be a champion in your local real estate market. You can be the superhero for your family. You just have to want it and take massive action.

I'm now approaching eight thousand transactions and a billion dollars in sales. Those numbers represent a lot of great accomplishments, feats and milestones. But they also represent a lot more mistakes and failures. You don't have to make the same mistakes that I've made. You don't have to take thirty-nine years to achieve at this level. *I can pass on more knowledge and information to you, probably, on the failures and the mistakes that I've made than on the successes.* I love sharing with other agents so that they can avoid the pain and suffering I've gone through to achieve at my level. I'm excited to be able to give back to my industry by helping others.

This industry has given me a magnificent life over the past thirty-nine years. Something I never dreamed was possible from a kid who grew up in an eight hundred square foot house. Three bedrooms, one bath, an unfinished basement, a gravel driveway, no garage, and eight people living in it. Imagine. Eight people vying for one bathroom. Someone who wore hand-me-downs all his years growing up. The accomplishments I've achieved, I didn't think were possible. The only way I thought that I could get into college was through my athletic abilities. My drive. My grit. The fire in my belly. That eye of the tiger. That's how I was going to get there. Taking my athletic abilities and working hard.

I worked for the government for a period of time, and I felt like their whole attitude and mindset was, "How much can we get away with while not doing a lot and still getting paid?" I just didn't resonate with that at all. I was the guy who went out and ran the mail route, and got it done in four hours instead of eight hours. As an example, when I first started with them, I was criticized for getting an eight-hour job completed in four hours. I was expecting a pat on the back, but instead, got criticized. That mindset was so foreign to me. So I moved on. From there, I got into the real estate industry, and like any new agent, I struggled.

Licensed in October 27 of 1977, I didn't have my first sale until February of 1978. I was buying Camaros and Firebirds one at a time (because they were the popular cars) and selling them and making five hundred dollars on each car, or a thousand dollars on a car, so I could pay my rent, pay on my charge cards, and pay back people that I was borrowing money from. It wasn't easy on the front end. It wasn't overnight success. It was a daily struggle managing myself. And yes, it was one day at a time. Beginning every day at zero. And I never lost faith. I never fell into inaction or paralysis, but kept moving, kept trying. I took action every day.

Final Words

I've worked my whole life to write this book. I've done a lot of research (painful research through trial and error and encountering every type of roadblock imaginable). Here I am, sitting down with pen and paper, contemplating how to wrap it all up. How do I influence other people's lives? I feel like I have something to contribute. I've had the privilege and the opportunity to be coached by some of the most magnificent players you could ever imagine. The best of the best. Some of these agents that I've shadowed are still at the top of the game in their franchises or in their independent companies all over the United States. They're still achieving at extraordinary high levels because they have that in them. They constantly try to get better at what they do. Personally, I feel that to be able to give that back to other agents in the industry is an enormous reward.

I'm coaching an agent right now who does fairly well. She has the passion and wants to perform at the highest level. She's probably over a half-a-million-dollar income earner and she has the ability to get to two million. I enjoy working with her and helping her, because I've been in that range. I've achieved nearly two million in gross commission income in a twelve-month period, and simultaneously led twenty agents to do a thousand transactions in twelve months. I've had that experience of selling a property almost every day for a year. Three hundred and fifty-one properties in three hundred and sixty-five days, and I took fourteen days off on a vacation. If I'd not taken the vacation I'd have hit that high number.

I sought education and growth through traditional education sources. Reaching out to Harvard's Negotiation Process course in Boston was a great experience for me in a course in negotiations. Being an owner of a company that had ten offices and about three hundred agents for four years, I believe that was an MBA program in and of itself. Life can be your school if you can learn from your experiences.

I've been in the real estate business for a long time now. I've had some successes, but I've had a whole lot more failures than I've ever had successes. If I succeeded with a thousand transactions in a year and a billion dollars in total sales volume, I guarantee I've lost a billion dollars in sales volume that I could have gotten if I'd been a little bit smarter at what I was doing. Out of almost 8,000 transactions I've had in real estate, I guarantee I've probably have lost seven or ten thousand transactions. You've got to learn how to get up and brush yourself off, and get back in the game. Some of these things, I'm beginning to learn how to master.

At the same time, I want to extend an invitation for you to come and shadow me. If you don't think that I'm the kind of real estate coach you'd like to hire to go to work for you, then don't hire me. If you do come and shadow me, and you don't think that you'll get your money's worth times ten from spending a day with me, then just say so. I'll give your money back. No questions asked. If not me, then seek a coach that works for you. Just make the decision to take action. Massive action.

When you're doing it because you love to do it, you're good at it, and you're still having fun at it, that's true happiness. I mean, even after 7,000 plus transactions, when I get a listing today, I still get that, "Yes!" feeling. Now, how do you maintain that? I have no desire to retire. Thirty-nine years, seven thousand transactions, nearly a billion in sales volume, and I have no desire to retire whatsoever. If nothing else, aren't you curious about how you maintain that level of excitement and enthusiasm for the industry that you're in? I don't know too many people that have done anything for thirty years that want to continue to do it with the same passion as their early days.

I guess I should get off my passionate rant and try to wrap it up for you. The key to personal power is the ability to take action on a consistent basis in the spirit and mindset of C.A.N.I. (Constant and Never-ending Improvement). Tony Robbins inspired me with this advice and I agree with it one hundred percent. The ability to take massive action on a consistent basis is the key to personal power. With the relentless quest for Constant and Never-ending Improvement.

Whether through you taking action by implementing two or three (or more!) ideas from this book or if you take *massive action* and come out to Dayton to shadow me, or hire me as a coach, I would like to motivate you and help you achieve your dreams as the ultimate success! I want to wish you a long and prosperous career doing what you love and are passionate about. I wish you a long career of taking action and continuous improvement... change for the good!

Appendix

A Career Retrospective: Phil's Top 5 Lists

"Winning isn't everything, but the
will to win is everything."

—Vince Lombardi

"It's not about the goal. It's about becoming the
type of person that can accomplish the goal."

—Tony Robbins

I love these two quotes. One is from one of my mentors, Tony Robbins. Both communicate an important ideal. As you are setting goals, accomplishing those goals is important. But if you find a way to accomplish a goal, but don't really improve and grow as a person, that is a hollow victory. Your personal quest for greatness isn't about winning awards, amassing wealth and riches, or getting accolades right and left. (That's the "Me" wall, remember?) Your goal is to become the best person you can be, to grow not only financially but also spiritually and academically, and grow in your capacity to be a caring, loving and involved human being. In this book, I've shared some of my growth, some of my challenges and some of my shortcomings. And most importantly, what I learned from them and now what you can learn from them.

As I was reviewing this book before sending it to the publisher, I felt there was something missing. I felt like it needed a type of summary, a type of recap of important points, vital life lessons and mistakes that I have learned along the way. I was looking for a type of road map and synopsis that was easily scanned, but that communicated big thoughts. That's why you are reading this appendix. It's my stab at adding what I felt was missing. Being a big fan of David Letterman's "Top Ten" lists, I came to the conclusion that this appendix would be in the form of a handful of "Top Five" lists.

I am constantly told that young people are impatient and won't take the time to read long passages of verbiage. I am not sure if that's correct, I am more optimistic about our younger generations and generations to come. I know that the Millennial generation is where our next real estate superstars are coming from. But that being said, the rise of social media where we communicate in 140 characters or less and we get our information from one-page Infographics that are a combination of images and words in short bite size nuggets, is a reality that we must adjust to. So, in a bit of an informal addition to the book, here is what I hope will be a helpful "Top Five" list that will attempt to encapsulate some of the ideas in this book.

My Top 5 Business Building and Money Making Ideas Incorporated into My Business

○ **Earning my CCIM License and opening up the commercial side of my business**

One day, my coach, Bob Bohlen called me and said, "Herman, go get your CCIM Designation," and hung up. Later, I was whining to him about how much work that would take (the Certified Commercial Investment Member designation is a very rigorous and intense program of courses and training that can take years to complete, and is considered by many to be the "Ph.D of Commercial Investment Real Estate). I also tried to argue how I was very happy working just residential real estate. Of course, he is my coach, so there was never any question what I was going to do. So, I enrolled, put my nose to the grindstone and earned the prestigious CCIM designation.

This little piece of advice has put millions of dollars in my pocket over the years. Basically, I was able to open a whole new income stream. And that has been a great boost for my career, my family and my business. All because I took the advice from my coach!

○ **Implementing a powerful Expired and FSBO (For Sale by Owner) campaign**

It started with a late-night brainstorm session in Craig Proctor's office in Toronto Canada on how to market to these two lucrative market sectors. It's been a powerful program and income stream for my business in the Dayton/Cincinnati region. Going after Expireds and FSBO's is nothing new; agents have always had their eyes on how best to tap into this market sector. What I did was put together a system and marketing plan that consistently and effectively targeted both Expireds and FSBO's. It's a comprehensive plan; remember, I have my courier collecting addresses whenever he sees a new FSBO. That little mechanism in our system has generated hundreds of thousands of dollars for our real estate business. Expireds are a different challenge.

Success here hinges on getting to them early and my powerful USP (Unique Selling Proposition) of being the number one agent in my area is a powerful and compelling angle to win that business.

○ **My $100 Visa Card office visit promotion/enticement offer**

This program has been a huge success for me. Basically, it's an offer that we bring out of our back pocket to entice a prospect to come out to the office for a 15-minute meeting or consultation. You've read the script earlier on how we use it. It's a powerful tool in our marketing arsenal. It lowers the objections for the prospect to come out and meet with me, and my closing rate is consistently high, so it's a win/win. Some agents have told me they could never afford to give $100 away to get a prospect to meet with them. Here's a nugget of advice: It's not good to get so caught up in the cost to generate that lead; it's more important to focus on the ROI, return on investment. If I use this mechanism to get 10 people in my office and I close six to seven of these (my closing ratio is higher), isn't that $1,000 investment a great investment? Let's use the low end of the spectrum and say the commission generated from each transaction is $6,000. Well that $1,000 investment got me $36,000 to $42,000 in commissions. Who wouldn't invest $1,000 with these returns? You'd be surprised at how many agents get so hyper focused on having to pay out $1,000 out of pocket and put on their blinders and don't take that "massive action" and make that bet. What's that old saying? It takes money to make money? Well, with my average closing ratio when I get in front of a prospect, the chances of me recouping that $100 investment with a closed transaction is pretty high. It might not be for every agent (if you are new and you haven't honed your closing skills, you may want to wait to implement this gem), but it's served my business well.

○ **Structuring my team's schedule so that every team member (even administrative) spends two hours of their day prospecting**

This program may not make sense to some agents and teams, but it's been a positively powerful benefit to our business model. I have a trademark business principle I adhere to, that I want *every* team member to cover their costs, and then after that to be a profit center unto themselves. It has been actually really really cool to watch some of my admin team members turn into really good telemarketers and sales people. And as I said, I can make a call and not get the appointment. Perhaps the call was made at a bad time of day when the person was trying to get their kids off to school. My admin might call later in the day, make a connection that I may not have been able to make, and she gets that appointment set. It also has created a great team synergy in the office. And remember, no single agent can match the power of a team united behind a common goal.

○ **Investing in my business by building a brand and then leveraging that brand through marketing and advertising**

To this day, I think one of the best decisions I have made was to find the best advertising and marketing agency in North America (specializing in real estate branding and marketing) and hire them to create a brand for me. It was 1988 and I contracted with Greg Herder and his agency to create a brand. Ever since, I've worked with them to find ways to leverage that brand to continue to grow my business.

I have always told other agents about the power of investing in their careers by building a brand. To me, it's reverse prospecting. When I am prospecting, I am calling people to ask them to do business with me. When I advertise my brand and leverage that brand, people are compelled to call me and ask me to do business with them. It's powerful. But so few agents make that investment. And you know me, always tweaking things, I found that when I married the power of a well-established brand with ninja telemarketing and prospecting efforts, the results have been amazing. You can have a successful career through marketing. You can have a successful career by getting on the phone constantly. When you supercharge the power of your daily prospecting with the leverage of a well-known brand, or brand name, it's amazing.

It's important to note that if you build a career without a brand, you are only able to chase and close leads that are hot right now. If you create a brand, it's working out in the market place for you 24/7, and people do call me and say, "we always knew we were going to use you when we were ready to sell, and now we are." I got on the *menu of agents* in their minds. If you do not have a brand and/or great name recognition, you most likely would never be on that client's mind/menu when they were selecting an agent. You are on a treadmill with a very limited number of leads and prospects to work from. As I stated earlier, without my investment to build and cultivate a brand, I may not have been where I am today, approaching 8,000 transactions and nearly 1 Billion Dollars in sales volume!

My Top 5 Ideas that Improved My Productivity and Efficiency, and Streamlined My Systems

○ **Implementing the CITO program**

The CITO program (Coming Into The Office) that I implemented was hands down the single biggest game changer in my career. When it comes to making my business operations more efficient (and my personal time and resources I spent in my business), it is the grand-daddy of efficiency ideas. I owe this one to my Coach, Bob Bohlen, and my Marketing Coach, Greg Herder. They simultaneously began urging me to make this radical change in my business. And you know what? I fought them tooth and nail. I was the ultimate naysayer to this idea. (The negative voice in my mind was on overdrive). I had one in each ear, one on the East Coast and the other on the West Coast, telling me how I would benefit from having my clients drive and come into the office to meet me as opposed to my routine of driving to their house and conducting a standard listing presentation. I swore up and down that homeowners would reject this, that going to the clients' houses was just how it was done. Boy, was I wrong.

Previously, I could do four listing presentations in an eight-hour day, *if* the locations were close enough to my office or each other, and *if* each meeting went quickly and efficiently. With all the driving from the office to the house, back to the office again, and then to the next appointment, in reality, it was more like two to three listing presentations a day—on a good day. Because I made this fundamental mindset shift and started inviting my clients to come into my office instead of me driving all over town, I can do four in an hour! This has freed up so much time for me to prospect and be the rainmaker. I am also more on top of my game, focused, and not tired from all that driving.

In addition, I am more in control when I do my presentation because it's on my turf with all my resources available to me. I also get to make a big impression with the quality of my office and staff and the professionalism on display. If you think about it, Doctors, Attorneys, CPAs and other professionals never come to your home. We as Realtors can command the same respect if we want it. This one really turned it around for me and my business operations!

○ **My yellow pad of accountability! Courtesy of Bob Bohlen**

This one seems simple enough, almost inconsequential. But it truly makes a difference in my productivity each and every day. On one of my many visits to shadow my coach, Bob Bohlen, I remember seeing him going about his business, but always picking up this mysterious yellow legal pad and referring to it. I asked him and he explained that it was his way of keeping his priorities listed and managed. It was his to-do list and all through the day he would refer back to that list and adjust the list to keep his priorities focused and make sure he got done what he needed to be done. He told me it helped him hold himself accountable to the list of items he has deemed to be his priorities. I took this idea from him and started my "yellow pad of accountability" back in my office in Dayton. It functions like a to-do list for me, but it's my way of managing what I should be putting my energies on, and making sure I get those items crossed off that list is my focus. I admit it's old school, but it works for me. It's like having a coach looking over my shoulder, as I am obsessed with getting those things on the list done in the priority order. That keeps me on track and productive.

○ **Incorporating the "Problem Form" into my real estate practice (Inspired by Allan Domb)**

When I was shadowing Top Producer, Allan Domb, in Philadelphia, I was struck by how he and his team kept referring to and utilizing a sheet they called "The Problem Form." As Allan and I sat talking about his operations, a team member would come in and ask for Allan's help. But unlike how my team and I interacted, they seemed to quickly resolve and process that employee's challenge. What a contrast to how I interacted with my team. I used to come into my office in the morning and walk a gauntlet. It started from the moment I walked in the door, and it was initiated by a harmless phrase, "Do you have a minute?" Well, it *never* was just one minute and that little daily ritual cost me big time, it ate up an hour or more of my day! One by one, my team approached (or sometimes, more like accosted) me with a series of challenges they needed help with, a decision they needed from me (oftentimes one they could have made), or an emergency they felt needed my immediate attention when many times it did not.

I watched how Allan and team interacted using this form. On this form was a quick, concise statement about what the specific issue was, then three to five important supporting points or background information. Allan was able to quickly scan the form and either advise the team member what they should do, or if it was too complex or above the pay grade of the team member, Allan would put that task into his DayTimer to do himself.

I took that form and implemented it in my office. What I found was that the amount of problems they had for me started to diminish. You see, some of the things being dumped on me were the result of a team member being lazy or subconsciously throwing the hot potato into my lap. Once they had to decide between taking the time to carefully fill out the form or just solving it themselves, they miraculously handled it themselves more times than not. Another reason for the decline of hot potatoes *thrown into Phil's court* was that when they filled out the form a couple of times and saw how I advised them to handle it, an amazing thing happened. They learned. They learned how to handle it on their own the next time it came around. I decided to change the name from "The Problem Form" to "The Solution Form," because it was forcing (or teaching) team members to find solutions. I have to tell you that this dramatically improved efficiency all around the office. It saved me time not having to be the problem solver. It saved time because my team started solving issues more efficiently and quickly. I can't put a dollar amount on the improvements, but I know it's in the hundreds of thousands of dollars saved over the years (based on my hourly rate and monies lost because I was a fireman putting out fires instead of being out there prospecting and being a rain maker.)

○ **Implementing the "stacked" office meeting process**

An off shoot of moving to the CITO method of listing presentations, this innovation is borrowed from how doctor offices function. What we did was schedule listing presentation meetings about 15 minutes apart. I instructed my team to have one client in Meeting Room 1, another family in Meeting Room 2, and then another prospective client in Meeting Room 3. And the next couple waiting in the lobby. Then I instructed my team on how to prepare a file for each client with key points that I could scan prior to walking in to the meeting, I had all my key talking points right there and I walked into that meeting prepared. I have been doing this real estate business for 39 plus years. I know what I am doing and my closing rate is pretty high. When this system is humming and they are stacked 4 deep, I am in my element. It's like a ballet; it's synchronized. This system, when it's working at full throttle is a thing of beauty!

○ **Implementing regular and robust "role playing" with my team and the power of scripts**

If you work in a Phil Herman real estate office, you will become familiar with role playing and training based on role playing. It's not uncommon for me to make a live prospecting call during an office meeting or training session. I want them to hear me, live, working without a net, so to speak. I will call a prospect and let them hear how I approach the script we've worked on, let them see how I overcome objections, how I work toward setting an appointment. It's even a learning experience to have them watch me crash and burn (it happens on occasion).

We'll also break into groups of two and take turns being the prospect and the telemarketer. Then we switch roles. It's the best way to get your team familiar with the scripts, so they don't sound like scripts. The goal is to make it second nature, almost like breathing. I always tell my team, if they know you're working a script, you're dead in the water. This type of culture and training environment has made the Phil Herman Team quite a formidable group of prospectors. It makes us better at what we do and we become an efficient, streamlined and knowledgeable sales unit.

My Top 5 Self Improvement Exercises, Rituals and Habits that Improve My Mental, Physical and Spiritual Well Being

○ **The "Kevin Costner Bull Durham" Focus Exercise**

There is a scene in the baseball-based movie, "Bull Durham," that really resonates with me. In the scene, Kevin Costner, who plays an aging pitcher out on the mound, goes through a process where he closes his eyes and slowly tunes out all the outside distractions: the crowd noise, the batter glaring at him, the organ music, and focuses all his being into that single next pitch. That's how I approach every listing appointment. I close my eyes and force out any distractions and any negative energy, and focus on that next 15 minutes. I clear the decks, all my worries, cares, frustrations, pain have to go away because I only have 15-20 minutes to get them to like me, trust me and feel like I can get the job done. To use that athlete analogy, all the sports heroes we admire do this. The level of their focus is titanic. Their ability to shut out the distractions of the outside world and focus on that single putt, that one pitch, that tennis serve, that basketball jump shot, is what makes them champions (backed by the countless hours of practice and Constant and Never-ending Improvement).

○ **Constantly blocking out the negative conversation in my mind and replace it with the positive**

I know that many agents will read my book and then the negative voices inside their head will take over. "I can't do a 15-minute listing presentation like Phil does." "I could never get clients to come to my office for a listing appointment." "I couldn't afford to spend $100 to get prospects in front of me, that's too much money!" I know, and I understand, because everyone has that negative voice playing in their heads.

When Greg Herder and Bob Bohlen were talking in each ear directing me to start doing CITO listing presentations, I had that voice in my head: "People would NEVER come to my office!!" "That's not how real estate is done." And I listened to those voices and could not pull the trigger on Bob and Greg's sage advice. It wasn't until one very harried and traumatic day where I was losing it and having a mid-day meltdown, and my office manager told me about setting up a listing appointment with two prospects that afternoon. I lost it. I told her "there is no way I can physically and mentally make it out there to their house this afternoon, ask them to come meet me at my office tomorrow, instead." Of course, in my mind, that exchange translated into *"I don't care if I lose that potential customer, I am too spent to even make the attempt."*

To my surprise, she called me back shortly thereafter and said, "They have agreed to come in and meet you." That's when the light switch went on, and the positive voices started overpowering the negative thoughts. *"Maybe this CITO thing CAN work!"* *"I think I can make this happen."* "Wow, *this is really going to work!"* If you listen to and succumb to that steady stream of self-doubt and negativity, it will take you down. If you don't think you can do something, you're right. If you think you can do something, you're right!

○ **Listen, learn and grow**

I am a voracious reader. These days, it's more audio books and TED Talks. I love being a sponge and soaking in all those new ideas and innovations. I have always been a student of the game, whether that's in life or business. Webinars, seminars, audio books, oh my! Feed the mind and grow the spirit.

○ **Take care of yourself**

Taking care of yourself, your physical body is vitally important. If you are in top fighting form physically, it helps you be in top fighting form mentally. I exercise religiously, I eat healthy (at one time I was on a macrobiotic and then a strict Vegan diet, but now I eat vegetarian) and I pay attention to my body and what it needs to be healthy. I also take care of my spiritual side. I make it a point to block out time each week for self-reflection, meditating, and listening to that positive voice in my head. Remember, it's all about Kaizen (Change for Good or for the

Better) and C.A.N.I. (Constant and Never-Ending Improvement) in your life. That's how you build a magnificent life and a magnificent business.

○ **Take care of others in your life**

It's amazing, but it happens all the time. People get so caught up in their goals, their business, their challenges and problems. This pulls all your focus away from the important people in your life. You absolutely need to take care of others in your life who are important to you. You can build a magnificent business and career, but if it costs you your relationships with important people in your life, that is a tragedy, pure and simple. Take the time to spend with your spouse. Remember simple little gifts. Listen to them, ask them how their day went. Spend time with your kids and be there for them. You are the most important influence in their lives. Make it count. Go on date nights. Schedule family nights. Put it on the calendar and treat it as the most important thing you can be doing at that moment. Those people who are close to you in life are your most important asset. Treat them like gold.

Top 5 Strategies and Action Steps for Building (and Keeping) a Successful Real Estate Team

○ Hire for Attitude and Train for Competence

Hiring talent is one of the most important action steps any business will do. Even though corporations have raised it to the level of a science these days, it's always going to be somewhat of a crapshoot. People put on their mask when they walk in the door for your interview, so you aren't always getting a true picture of who that person is, and more importantly, how they will mesh, gel, and interact with your team. Your team has a chemistry. It's either locked in and very stable like the "Noble Gases" in the periodic table in chemistry, or it can be highly unstable where just the slightest wrong catalyst can create instant chaos. Don't hire that unstable element that will throw all your hard work on your team out the door. Yes, it's very important to hire the most experienced person for that specific role, and you must carefully review that candidate's resume, references and job history. It's a balance. Good personality and great background/experience. But that being said, I've learned through painful trial and error that it is always better to hire for *attitude*. That is, you want a good personality and fit for your team over a highly experienced candidate who could be a poison pill that could take the morale and drive of your team down the tubes with a toxic personality. Some of my best, most important team members who have been with me the longest, have been people who weren't super experienced, but I loved their attitude. The energy they brought to my team far outweighed any lack of experience. Remember, you can train a person to do a task or perform a role, but you can't train a Negative Nelly to be a Positive Patty. It can be done, but they are more than likely hardwired that way, and the energy you spend trying to correct this behavior is time you are not building your business. Remember, your team is like your family away from your family. Hire people you will want to be around.

○ Interviewing Strategies

I'm always asked what interviewing strategies I use to build my high performing team. I've built several teams, dismantled others, and constantly have to hire and replace because life happens and people move on. Per a recommendation by my coach Bob Bohlen, I use a service called Caliper Profile (CaliperCorp.com) to help construct my interview questions and processes. Beyond that, after going through the first impression stage (how are they dressed, appearance, manners and yes, hygiene), my key strategy is to greet them, introduce myself, and then just let them talk.

Listening is most important at this time. I ask them to tell me about themselves, their life story, where were they born, where did they go to school, hobbies, and job experience. I just let them talk while I listen. But, *really listen*. We all have a habit of half-listening, thinking of what our next question will be, etc. Listen to what they are saying and how they are saying it. Then make your best choice. Sometimes you are in a bind and you need someone fast. Just be judicious. Remember the old business adage, Hire Slowly. Fire Fast. It's far too common in the world of business that companies drag their feet when dealing with a bad or disruptive employee. So, take your time selecting, but get rid of the poison pill quickly (of course, while adhering to basic HR guidelines and laws and making sure you are legally covered).

○ Incentives (The Science of Motivation and the Art of Inspiring)

Incentivizing is a very critical part of keeping and inspiring your team so that it is performing at peak level and firing on all cylinders. There are two strategies to get any team to perform. The carrot (rewards to get performance) or the stick (pain and punishment for not performing, or the "non-reward"). There are different opinions on this, but sometimes you need both. Focusing too much on the "stick" can backfire on you and your team. I personally try to hire people who don't need negative reinforcement, and then focus on finding the right balance of positive incentives.

Some goals are big (like our 100 set appointments in 30 days) and require big incentives (my team dinner with $1,000 cash and two hours to spend it). Some are smaller and require smaller incentives. It's important to gauge that, because if you over incentivize, you have to keep upping the ante, which gets expensive. If you under-incentivize, you potentially get poor team performance. A couple of points that have helped me are: First, sometimes money is a great motivator. Sometimes it's not. The key is to try and drill down and find out what's important to your team or team member. For instance, one team member might be motivated by cash, but the most important thing for them might be the flexibility to pick up their child from school, and if you gave them a flexible schedule to accomplish this, you would see them move mountains to get that.

Find each member's personal goals and passions and try to incentivize to those. Dr. Fred Grosse, one of my advisors over the years, taught me the "10-25-50-100" sliding scale of incentivizing strategies. This is important for your team and will also work for yourself. The strategy is to have incentives at various levels to reward certain accomplishments. A small accomplishment might be worth 10 "points." Things such as getting an appointment set up, accomplishing a small or nagging task you needed to do, might be worth a 10-point prize. This might be treating yourself to Frappuccino, or my personal favorite, a hot tea with honey. A little bit bigger goal might be worth 15 points, and it might be treating yourself to some time away from the office to read your favorite book. A 25-point goal and reward might be worth treating your significant other to a nice dinner and movie, to spend a lovely evening with someone important in your life. A 50-point goal might be rewarded by buying a new car. Really larger goals, like hitting financial milestones, or something large might be worth 100 points, and it might be building your dream home or taking a dream vacation to Fiji.

Take the time to ask your team players what is important to them, to spell out what might be a good reward for these various levels of accomplishment. Have them write it out, in fact. Then set up your reward system and goal structure. One of my key team players, Brian, is an avid cyclist. His 50-point reward might be a beautiful Italian carbon fiber bicycle. His big reward might be a trip to see the Tour de France. The incentivizing of your team is very important and you should devote a sufficient amount of time to structure this. Never do this haphazardly. You'll either over incentivize or under incentivize your team, affecting their performance. I suggest you block out sufficient time to structure this. It's critical to your team's overall performance. And it's a vital component in your endless quest to maximize the retention of your team. Retention has a huge effect on your bottom line, you know how detrimental it is to have to take your focus off what's important (prospecting and being the rain maker) in order to find and train a new team replacement.

In regards to how and when to use the "negative" or "non-reward" incentive strategy, here is an interesting side note on the subject of how I work with *my* personal real estate coach. He is a master of setting up just the right incentives, including a little strategic use of the "stick" approach. Bob called me one day, and in his mode of *Chief Accountability Officer* in my business/career, he asked me, "Herman, how are you doing on making your calls to sellers and getting listing extensions and price reductions and servicing your clients?" Well, I often used creative avoidance in making these calls. I hated them. They made me uneasy. Getting a price reduction from the seller is critical in helping them get to the right pricing strategy and getting their home sold. (Note: later when I moved aggressively to using the independent appraisal strategy to determine the pricing of the home vs. wrestling with the seller to pull a price out of the air, this cut down on the number of price reduction calls.) I stammered and Bob knew I was in avoidance mode. He said, "Herman, take out your check book and write a check to me for $50,000. You have three days to finish up those calls. If you hit your goal, I'll tear up that check. If you don't, I'll have fun cashing it!"

Well, I was panicking, to say the least. I was so afraid that I might not get a single price reduction in the allotted 72 hours. I rallied my team and we hit the pavement hard and were able to get the 15 price reductions in 48 hours, much to my (and my bank account's) relief. There was a reward side to hitting that goal that I can't seem to remember, but the non-reward was so intimidating that it motivated me like crazy. In the back of my head, I was terrified of having to tell my wife that I wrote a $50,000 check to Bob to spend as he pleased!

Another personal example of this non-reward strategy involved my other mentor, Dr. Fred Grosse, Ph.D Business Psychologist. He taught me that we as humans will do more to avoid pain than we will do to gain pleasure. To help me in reaching a personal goal, he told me to put up $1,000 on the line. If I reached the goal, I was to reward myself with a $1,000 shopping spree. If I failed and didn't accomplish the goal, I agreed to his recommendation that I would write a $1,000 check to my main competitor to use against me in his marketing. If you know how much I hate to lose, you'd know that I hit that goal.

○ Role Playing in Training

I've spoken extensively about this previously. It's a common training strategy in the business world, and it should also be utilized in your training sessions with your team. They may need some coaxing and teaching to get up to speed on how to do effective role-playing, but I think it's invaluable. Schedule these sessions regularly. Get your team dialed in and super comfortable with your scripts, they need to know it like the back of their hand so that the prospects never feel like they are listening to a script. When your team feels confident and prepared then they will enjoy their work more, perform at a higher level, and when the whole team is firing on all cylinders, the synergy can be explosive. And that is another component to help your retention efforts.

○ Instilling a "pride of ownership" mindset in my team

This is a minor item, but I think still important. I mentioned earlier that when I walk the office, I am not afraid to stop and pick up a piece of trash on the lobby floor. I will replace a paper towel roll in our kitchen. If I take pride in the appearance of our office, it is infectious to the rest of the team. I instill that pride in the whole team. And it goes beyond just the appearance of the office interior. It's also about the "face" the team puts up for our clients, prospective clients and vendors we interact with. I want every team member to be enormously proud of how we carry ourselves, and our appearance, our manners and responsiveness to people we encounter in day-to-day business operations. Word of mouth can be your biggest business booster or your worst nightmare. When people think of the Phil Herman Real Estate Team, I want it to be in superlatives: the best, the greatest, the most-friendly, most responsive. Think of the Ritz Carlton mindset we referenced earlier. I know that if they are thinking this, they will communicate that to their friends, relatives and business associates. This dramatically impacts our bottom line, and more importantly, this pride of ownership in your team will do wonders in attracting and keeping the best performers. Winners want to play on a winning team with other winners. So keep the losers out of the equation when building, maintaining, and retaining your real estate team!

Top 5 Reasons Why You Must Hire a Real Estate Coach

○ **Accountability, accountability, accountability!**

I've said it before and I'll say it again: **The definition of a Coach is someone to hold you accountable to do what you don't want to do in order to get you what you *do* want to attain.** The truth is, left to our own devices we find creative ways to avoid the hard work and discipline we need to grow our business. This is the most important role a coach will play in your life and business. I know some people will fight that, they will not want to be held accountable. That's human nature. But I also know that there are many people who will embrace that because they truly want to rise above. If you reject accountability, you are not a good candidate for coaching. You are also not a good candidate to reach incredible levels of success. The choice is yours.

○ **Perspective, perspective, perspective**

A good coach, especially one who is still in the game (and not a real estate "*has been*" or wash out, or he/she was an agent long ago and out of touch with *today's* challenging market), will be able to provide you the all-important perspective you need to succeed. In the corporate world, they coach CEO's to regularly take time out to view their business from a 10,000-foot perspective. The analogy is to take a helicopter ride up to be able to look down on the overall big picture of your operations. If you don't, you are in the weeds, embroiled in the grind of your day-to-day struggle to run a real estate business. You know that things can get hairy. The waters can get rough. If you are consumed, both physically and mentally, on solving the latest problems, putting out the latest fires that have popped up, you cannot make incisive and insightful career decisions. Or worse, you fail to even do any career planning or growth. In the book, *The E-Myth*, it warns of getting into a scenario where you are working *in* your business and not working *on* your business.

A coach will play an invaluable role here, helping you to get that 10,000-foot overview/perspective on your business. They will help you work on your business. And if you are working with a coach who is still in the game, they will actually help you with the forest fires and problems that you might run into as well, because they have lived that themselves. That's not their focus, but it's a fringe benefit of working with a coach who is still an active and successful agent. That's what Bob Bohlen did for me.

○ **Help you set goals and serve as your personal board of advisors**

When you have made the decision that you want to take your career to the next level and you understand that a coach is the way to help you get there, then one of the most important benefits they can do for you is to help you establish the right goals to pursue, something that is very hard to do because you are too close to your business. The danger is that agents often set goals that are unrealistic, too low, too high, or even the wrong thing that they should be focusing on. With a coach, you aren't going it alone. You have a sounding board, it's almost like having a board of advisors you can turn to with problems or turn to when seeking advice.

○ **Cheerleader and Chief Inspiration Officer**

Life and business is a long and grueling process. Sometimes it's like a long hike. Sometimes it's like you are a prizefighter in the ring battling a tough opponent and it's the 11th round, and you are fading fast. It definitely feels like a full contact sport sometimes. When you have someone in your corner, it makes the going easier. It gives you the inspiration to keep plugging away. To keep the good fight going. We know in sports, when a team is playing at home, with the friendly hometown crowd cheering them on, it's easier to eke out a win. It's easier to mount a tough come back. When they are playing on the road, it's more like you are swimming upstream. You can't underestimate what an effect having a cheerleader in your corner can do to your career trajectory.

○ **Don't get your head handed to you on a plate. Know when to bob and when to weave. A coach can help you develop the best game plan to succeed.**

The real estate business is a highly competitive field, and it's only going to get more and more complex and competitive. Signs all point toward the rise of mega agents grabbing big chunks of market share, as well as real estate *teams and groups* that serve as small little real estate corporations. These are strong, business-minded groups and individuals who are hungry and aggressive. They are coming for your business or your clients. If you are truly passionate about your craft and profession, and you want to excel in the face of this rising tide, a coach is exactly what you need to not only do battle and survive, but to beat them at their own game. A savvy real estate coach who has achieved a high level of success himself or herself, can help you battle for market share and set up best practices in your business model. They will help you set up the systems to more efficiently handle increased growth and service more clients with less of your time and involvement. The best defense is a great offense. A coach who is active and still in the game can help you win this war and take your career to new levels.

List #6

Top 5 Mistakes I've Made in My Life and How I Learned to be a Better Person and Professional After Making Them

○ **Being petty, short sighted and thinking small**

In life, sometimes we are guilty of being petty, jealous and small minded. It's human nature. I made this mistake often in my life, but I've strived to minimize this. Think about the example I referenced in regard to the $100 gift card offer. Being small minded, an agent might say that he or she could never spend that much money on a promotion. But if they don't do the math and calculate their potential ROI on it, they could be costing themselves so much more in lost revenue that would dwarf their $100 cost.

Think about your day-to-day real estate business. Have you ever seen a transaction implode because of a simple request (such as the buyer asking for a money to cover a bad or faulty refrigerator)? When I was coming up as a rookie agent, one of my early mentors, Pat Mc-Gowan, who was a successful insurance agent, shared with me a great idea. He told me that I needed to set up a "slush fund." That is, set aside some money to allow you to take action to save a transaction. If the buyer is threatening to sue or derail a transaction because the refrigerator in the house sucks, pull the money out of your slush fund and buy a refrigerator to make that problem go away. The idea here is to try and rise above the muck and pettiness and to keep rising. So set up a personal slush fund, and change your mindset to avoid being small minded and petty. You should always strive to avoid this common human foible. Small minds will never accomplish big goals.

○ **Letting my ego control my destiny**

I'm just like everyone else—ego is important to me. But the mistake is when I let my ego affect me in adverse ways. This is a constant battle. I was wise enough to remove the "Me Wall" in my office. I have to make sure I don't get too full of myself where I think I know better than everybody. The more successful you become, the more susceptible you become to this trap. I shudder when I think of all the efficiency and potential income I lost when my ego told me I knew better than Bob Bohlen and Greg Herder when they told me to change my business model and move toward CITOs and conduct the bulk of my listing presentations in the office. I let my ego control me. I knew better and I was absolutely positive that this would never work.

I used to let my ego affect me in our office meetings. I would summarily dismiss an idea from one of my team members because, *"I'm Phil Herman. What could you possibly know that I don't know?"* When this happened, I wasn't open to some great ideas that my team members (who are on the front lines with clients and vendors) would come up with. Some of these ideas (that I used to just flat out reject, or just give lip service to) have dramatically affected our bottom line and saved us money or generated income streams.

Another way my ego would cost me in my early days was thinking that certain leads or business opportunities were beneath me. One day, I watched one particularly arrogant agent turn up his nose at a lead that came in. I think he may have even laughed. It was a woman who wanted to sell a 400-square foot house, when at the time it was a $17,000 property. Well, I took that lead. I overcame my ego and went for it. I decided I would help this person. After all, I am in the people business. Well I am glad I didn't let my ego get the best of me. After helping this lady sell that home, I sold her a condo and she referred her father to me and I helped him sell six investment properties! That arrogant agent may have thumbed his nose at that lady's business, but I was able to help a person with their immediate need, and it turned out to be very lucrative for me down the road.

○ **Letting fear control my destiny**

Early in my rise in the world of Dayton real estate, I managed to become a partner in the most prestigious and largest realty firm in the area. It was a crowning achievement that I took great pride and satisfaction in. I thought to myself, "I've really made it. Surely, it doesn't get any better than this!" Well, a funny thing started to happen. My success was starting to threaten the other partners. In addition, they struggled with my branding campaign where I was branding myself so prominently (I had just started launching this in my business) and I think they didn't like that my branding was attempting to elevate me to the same level as the company branding and reputation. To them, it was all about their company and they didn't like that I was on the cutting edge of a new trend where individual agents were branding themselves and the company brand took a back seat to the individual agent's branding. Heritage is a good company. We just had different philosophies.

They forced the issue and threatened to ask me to leave. They told me I could not be successful outside "their umbrella." I listened to the negative thoughts in my head that said, "Maybe they are right!" I started to believe they were right. I had 70 active listings at the time. If I left, would I lose all that business? I was under great stress and duress trying to decide what to do. Should I leave and go out on my own, or cave in and toe the company line? For a moment, I was starting to buckle under that pressure and that fear that they might be right. Also, there were huge financial ramifications involved. Those 70 listings (70 potential pay days) were on the line. Because Ohio state laws and regulations stipulated that I would have to alert all those home owners/ listing clients about any potential move to another company, and that seller/listing client would have to sign papers to move their listing to my next company, I struggled with that negative bomb going off in my head. What if the owners were right that I needed their umbrella? What if the listing clients would agree and decide to keep their listing with the company (a highly respected business entity) rather than follow me to a lesser-known company? I agonized over this, and almost caved in to the fears. But something in my mind told me it would be better to take the gamble and make the move.

I am glad that I didn't succumb to my fears and let those fears determine my destiny. You know what, I made the decision to leave and it was the best decision. 95% of those listing clients agreed to move their listings with me and my next company. (I moved first to a local

RE/MAX office and then eventually to my own RE/MAX franchise.) And I now had the unfettered freedom to reach new heights in my career. I learned that real estate, like most service-based businesses, is a people business built on relationships. Those homeowners placed their trust in me, not so much in the company behind me. I learned that if you can shoot a 10-foot jump shot on your basketball court, you can make that shot on any basketball court.

So, I almost made the mistake of letting my fear determine my life decision, but I luckily avoided it. The rest became history, so to speak, as I supercharged my trajectory toward 7,000 transaction sides, well on my way to 8,000! If I had caved and stayed at that company and dropped my personal branding, I may not have reached the same heights I have reached!

○ **Not knowing the fine line between hard work and burnout**

I have always been hungry. During my wrestling days, and now my real estate career, I wanted to win —and win big. I was never afraid to put in the hard work and pay my dues. Besides, when you are passionate about what you do, the danger is that you lose sight of balance in your life. It didn't seem like work to me, and I enjoyed it so much! I started telling myself, "if working six days a week was great, then working seven days a week would be fantastic!" That was my mindset back in the day. In fact, I worked 16 hours a day for six years. I became one with my work. But after a while, I became aware that I was paying a price. I noticed that my efficiency was only at 60%. I lost my sharpness. I was suffering mental fatigue, not only from the sheer number of hours, but from the sheer monotony of only doing real estate. I had to get out of the trees so that I could more effectively see the forest (big picture).

I forced myself to pull back, to find more life balance. I found that I was now able to recharge my batteries. After making that life change, when I was in the game, I was in the game. I was in the moment (remember the Bull Durham Focus exercise? It came during this revelatory crossroads in my career). I learned the importance of life balance, and I urge you to not lose sight of this either!

○ **Dwelling on personal and professional setbacks, not pushing forward quickly enough**

It's important to realize that life is a journey, not a destination. You make strides; you make mistakes. Sometimes you take two steps forward, then get knocked one step back. The key is that if you fall down, you get back up, dust yourself off, and jump back on that road to continuous improvement. Trust me, I have been knocked down and buckled at the knees a few times in my life. The critical point is, "who are you going to be in the face of that pain and suffering?" In the darkest moments of *my* life, such as feeling mentally defeated as a young, aspiring wrestler, sinking to the depths of despair in my career when I was being asked to leave, and other dark periods, I have been buckled at the knees, devastated. My mistake was dwelling on the setback, allowing myself to be mired in the despair of the moment. But luckily for me I was pretty resilient, and this was only a temporary state. I was a fighter and I knew how to turn things around and right the sinking ship. I knew I could find a way out of the darkness, I only wish I acted faster.

You see, while this book is all about taking your career and your life to new levels of greatness and happiness, you will undoubtedly encounter *valleys* of darkness and despair in addition to the *peaks* of happiness and success. It's how you deal with those times that will really define you. For me, if I'm buckled at the knees, then I am also on my knees praying for guidance and clarity. If you are a spiritual or religious person, praying is one of the tools you have to lift yourself out of your darkness. If you are not a spiritual person, then you have to deal with that person in the mirror. Who will you be in those times? What kind of character will you display, how do you rise up from the ashes? It's up to you to find the people and resources to help you take the steps out of the depths and rise up and get back on the road to continuous and never-ending improvement.

To perfectly frame this book, I'll take you back to the beginning and the first chapter where I talk about the need for all of us to rely on others to really succeed in life. In your personal life, you have your loved ones, your family, your friends, your teachers, your pastor and religious leaders to help you. You have your prayers and spiritual side to get you through. Turn to these important people for advice, guidance or just a kind or encouraging word at the right time when you need it most.

The same applies to your professional life. One of my favorite sayings is "You're in business *for* yourself, not *by* yourself." There are so many resources for you to draw from for help, guidance and support. You aren't condemned or banished to do it all by yourself. Read articles from respected authors, take educational courses, webinars and workshops from trusted experts. Better, you can learn from agents who are more successful than you. Remember, a big part of my success was shadowing those 30-40 top agents. I plundered their good ideas and their great systems and took those ingredients and put them into my own cake of success. As one of my mentors, Dr. Fred Grosse, articulated it: Life is primary, work funds life. We must focus on dollar productivity and create a magnificent life. He states that we were born to live like royalty, there is no honor in poverty. You have *permission* to excel and succeed in life, you just need the personal *desire* to take massive action to make it happen.

And one of the biggest action steps you can take is to hire a personal real estate coach. If you are really serious about your success and career trajectory, the most direct route to success is to hire a great real estate coach. A good coach *will help you do what you don't want to do so that you can achieve what you want to achieve.* Find a coach who is an agent who knows what you are facing, who is navigating the current real estate market and overcoming the hurdles and obstacles of today's market. Not the market from 10 years ago. A coach who dabbled in real estate or who did it 5-10 years ago is not in touch with your world and the problems you face. Trust me, what agents faced even two years ago is quite different than what today's agents face.

I cannot even begin to stress how instrumental my coach, Bob Bohlen, was in my success. Just like me, he was out there doing battle and building his magnificent business and career at the same time I was (he was just so much further along than I was). When he advised me, I trusted his advice and knew he was speaking from experience garnered in the current real estate arena. His guidance and teachings helped shorten the learning curve. That is an incredibly invaluable benefit from working with a coach, and it can save you years of pain and learning by trial and error.

As I have mentioned, I am coaching a limited number of agents because I want to give back to this industry that has been so wonderful to me, my family and my life. I am extending an invitation to all serious agents out there like you who are ready to build their own magnificent career and life. Contact me if you are ready to take your career to the next level (Phil@PhilHermanCoaching.com). You want to look at that person in the mirror and know you are striving to be the best you can be, don't you?

It is my sincere hope that you will take the words and ideas in this book and strive to avoid the same mistakes I made. I wish you much success on your personal journey! Kaizen! Change for the good or better. That is your new mantra!

About the Author

"I have no desire to retire. If I live to be 100, I'm going to be working on that 100th day. Now, it doesn't equal or mean that I'm going to be working as hard as I worked in the past. What it does equal or mean is that I want to remain relevant and viable; a contributor."

Phil Herman, Realtor® Real Estate Coach

For Phil Herman, the long and winding road to becoming the top real estate professional in the Dayton/Cincinnati, Ohio area, as well as a Nationally renowned agent, has taught him volumes. On the road to closing nearly 8,000 transactions throughout his 30 plus year career, Phil has gleaned a lot of knowledge and learned many life lessons. And along the way, he learned a lot about real estate.

Some of those lessons were, indeed, hard and painful, but they were always approached with an upbeat attitude and a "success is not a destination, it's a never-ending journey" mindset. With this perspective on life, Phil has strived to be the best father to his son, Taylor, and the most effective resource to his clients who depend on him for one of life's most important investments.

Humble Beginnings

Phil—one of six children born into a working-class family—learned early on that anything worth attaining was worth working hard to achieve. In high school he struggled to make the wrestling team. Phil was unhappy; he expected more from himself, he wanted to contribute more to the team. But the other wrestlers seemed much faster and stronger. He took a job bagging groceries after school to earn tuition to top wrestling clinics. With hard work and determination, it wasn't long before he was in the top of his field, even winning 32 consecutive matches his senior year.

Personal Best

This boyhood story provides a keen insight into what makes Phil tick. With high expectations for himself, he sets his sights on a goal and works hard at doing whatever it takes to achieve it. It's a matter of constantly striving for his personal best in everything he does. It's Phil's nature to want to succeed. It's sheer determination and discipline that propel him there.

Fulfilling Career

Prior to becoming Dayton's top agent, Phil served in the military (the Marines) and then attended Ohio University, where he started cultivating his passion for business. On the recommendation and advice of a mentor, Pat McAllister, Phil took a temporary position in a local real estate firm. However, his quick aptitude and enthusiastic drive quickly pushed him to the top. He had found a career where he was a natural; his personable nature, his disciplined work ethic, and his sharp business sense earned him a place as a frontrunner in his field. What started out as a temporary position turned into a long and fulfilling career.

A Stellar Career

Quite simply, it has been quite an illustrious career. In his best year, he did 358 transaction sides with a small support team. That same year, he was also coaching and leading a team of approximately 15 agents, and as a group under Phil's tutelage, they did a combined 1,000 transaction sides that year. Phil had a single month where he did 47 transactions. That next month, he did another 43! That's 90 transactions in a 60-day period. He has outsold nearly 3,000 Dayton area agents 27 years straight. He is now approaching 8,000 transactions. Phil has been ranked in the top 100 Agents in the Nation 3 years in a row, as well as being featured in several real estate magazine profiles. He is an international speaker, constantly invited to share his insights with agents all over the world. Phil is regularly sought out by other top agents to learn the Phil Herman Method, to pick up their own career building ideas and tips. Phil also coaches agents one on one.

Kaizen and C.A.N.I.

Behind Phil's amazing career trajectory has been his belief in "Kaizen," a philosophy of "Change for Good" through constant learning. C.A.N.I. (Constant and Never Ending Improvement) is the driving force behind Phil's amazing success story and stellar real estate career. For Phil, it's also the essence behind his coaching style and philosophy when he works one-on-one with agents he coaches. He instills in his students this philosophy and shows them how to get on a path of "constant improvement" AND more importantly, how to make it into a permanent mindset. "Growth has to be a constant process," explains Phil. "If not growing daily and self-examining yourself to make sure you are committed to that daily growth, your skills, your execution and implementation will atrophy."

Phil works hard to help his coaching students adapt this mindset and approach to life and take their career trajectory as far and as high as they want to take it.

If you are curious about working with a coach to take your business to the next level, visit Phil's real estate coaching site at
www.PhilHermanCoaching.com
today.

Made in the USA
Middletown, DE
21 February 2022

61490857R00102